PURPOSELY POSITIVE

PURPOSELY POSITIVE

How to Live an Intentional and Inspired Life

JOEL LINDEMAN D.C.

TABLE OF CONTENTS

PURPOSELY POSITIVE
AN INTRODUCTION

"Life is like a room, and we are the painters. You can either choose to paint your room bright or dull, but always remember it is where you will always sleep."

—TERRY MARK

First off, THANK YOU for taking a step toward living your ideal life. Thank you for getting out of your comfort zone to live your life with intention, instead of just passing through it. Thank you for realizing there is so much more potential contained within the seeds of your existence than you have let blossom so far. Thank you for accepting the call to be more impactful. The world needs more people to wake up, take charge of their lives, and create a more positive present and lasting legacy. Thank you for deciding to do as Ghandi said and *"be a change you want to see in the world."-Mahatma Ghandi.*

And now let's get to work.

Did you know that the human brain is hardwired to be more negative than positive? Ever since humans walked on two legs (and more than likely, even before then), our brains have continually worked to avoid punishment and move toward reward. Unfortunately, punishments—negative experiences, pain, Uncle Borgo getting devoured by a lion, etc.—leave a much deeper impression on our minds than rewards do.

From generation-to-generation, certain attributes are passed on, such as hair color, eye shape, knobby knees, etc. But there are other non-physical things that get passed on as well. Knowledge and capacity for learning is woven throughout our family tree, and that tree prospered, creating more and more branches because our ancestors figured out how to avoid certain dangers and shared that knowledge with future generations. Sure, they also passed on things, like how to make the best rodent stew and where to find the tastiest grubs, but those lessons didn't have as much of an impact as the warnings did, such as how to run from predators and why it's important to be careful around crocodiles.

We were taught from generation-to-generation that life can be quite dangerous and we should therefore act accordingly. Being cautious may have stopped some leaps from occurring, but being vigilant also kept our DNA thriving in the gene pool, and that's why our brains are always on the lookout for negativity.

Believe it or not, there is a plethora of research on this topic. In a study conducted by John Cacciopo, Ph.D,[1] people were shown various pictures designed to stir up different emotions. There were two positive, two negative and thirty-six neutral photographs. The researchers then recorded the participant's brainwave activity with each image. The results showed a greater surge in brain activity following the viewing of a negative image compared to when looking at a positive one. The participants' brains were more active, more primed for the "bad" things than the "good" ones.

Another study in *The Journal of Experimental Psychology: General*[2] found that people are more likely to assume negative intentions of another person rather than positive ones.

---

1. Ito Tiffany, Larsen Jeff, Smith Kyle, Cacioppo John. "Negative Information Weighs More Heavily on the Brain: The Negativity Bias in Evaluative Categorizations": *Journal of Personality and Social Psychology* 75.4 (1998): 887-900.
2. Gawronski, B., Rydell, R. J., Vervliet, B., & De Houwer, J. (2010, October 4). Generalization Versus Contextualization in Automatic Evaluation. *Journal of Experimental Psychology: General. Advance online publication.* doi: 10.1037/a0020315

Pain is a great teacher, and the lessons learned last longer than the lessons learned from chocolate or certificates of merit. We have a 'negativity bias,' meaning we lean more toward negative perspectives and take larger actions based on negative instances than positive ones. Since we all have this bias, our brains are constantly seeking out warning signs, and negative information is soaked up like a sponge. Our brains are pushing us toward fear on an almost constant basis.

In order to combat this, you need to be vigilant in creating and noticing positive experiences, thoughts and memories. You need to actively work to pursue and attract positivity into your life. You need to strive to bring forth positive interactions, create positive atmospheres, and push yourself to learn, grow, motivate and inspire.

The purpose of this book is to arm you with ways to do exactly that.

This book is NOT designed to motivate you. There is a vast difference between motivation and INSPIRATION. Throughout this journey, the focus will be on the latter.

I mean no disrespect to any motivation you achieve, or any seminars you have been to, because they most definitely serve a great purpose. I work on my motivation daily. I listen to some amazing motivational speakers, read motivational quotes and books, and watch motivational videos. I simply want to differentiate between motivation and inspiration.

Motivation is like a bonfire, full of energy and raring to go. There is a place for that type of pyrotechnics in life, for sure. Inspiration, in contrast, is a slow-burn—a smoldering-coal-fire kind of heat. Inspiration is much more soothing and longer lasting; it warms and comforts the soul. Inspiration is more about awakening what's already there, and fanning the small flames that are burning right now—which keeps them burning longer—rather than forcing it with a match, lighter fluid, gasoline, or hair spray, which will eventually go out.

In this book, you will explore many aspects of your soul, and I use the word "explore" with great purpose. Exploration implies adventure, discovery, a journey into the unknown (or maybe just the sort-of-known). In order to truly get in touch with your purpose and keep your inspiration "furnace" burning—for your own good and the good of all humanity—you need to be willing to move into uncharted territory. You must ask new questions, seek new answers, and investigate the terrain of your life quite differently than you have been. This book will aid you in making more inspired decisions around living an intentional, purposeful life.

In picking up this book, you undoubtedly conducted an interview of sorts. Maybe you are glancing through this chapter at the bookstore in the airport or reading the description on Amazon and thinking, "Who is this Joel guy and why in the bloody hell should I listen to him?" First off, I can promise you this: I am not a Master of Mentality, Prince of Purpose, Emancipator of Emotion, or Sultan of Some-Cool-Word-That-Begins-With-S. But my soul and my spirit tell me I have work to do in this world, and a large portion of that job description entails sharing inspiration with others as best I can.

I have devoted a large portion of my life to understanding the human condition more deeply. I studied Psychology, Biology, Sociology, Biochemistry and Physiology on my way to earning a Bachelor's degree in Kinesiology and then a Doctor of Chiropractic degree afterward. I've continued my learning endeavors through numerous post-graduate courses over the past fifteen years. I've read (and continue to read) hundreds of books on the mind, personal growth, motivation and inspiration. I've attended numerous lectures on these subjects as well.

I've also experienced friends who have lived lives and deaths of "quiet desperation." I've seen firsthand the devastation that living a life without purpose can do to one's soul, and the souls of their loved ones. I've personally dealt with debilitating depression, low self-esteem, and entertained thoughts of ending it all in my past. I also, on occasion, have watched the news, and I understand that in order to create a better world for ourselves and for future generations, there is work to be done.

If you want to live your best life, you must take more command of it. You must put in the work to live your life more purposefully.

I also know that you are worth the work, and the people you interact with in your life are definitely worthy of the results of that work. Be prepared to go deep and to illuminate your soul. This isn't only to "figure yourself out," but to find out how you can wake up each day and feel like you are on the right path, inspired from within and living purposefully.

My hope is that throughout this journey, you will realize you have a plethora of choices at any given moment in your life. You can decide to revert to negativity, or you can intentionally choose to allow each moment (good or bad) to spur you on to a more vibrant future.

At the beginning of each chapter, there are words of wisdom to inspire you and provide insight into what to expect from the work ahead. There are also Purposely Positive Exercises (or PPEs, for short because who doesn't like acronyms) following each chapter. These are designed to help you investigate each topic further. These exercises are tools that will allow you to put this book into action.

And if you do, it will allow you to live with intention and bring forth the very best version of yourself.

PURPOSELY POSITIVE EXERCISE: SET YOUR INTENTION

All good things have a purpose behind them, so take five minutes to do the following:

- What do you want to change in your life?—Make a list of everything you'd like to change.

- From the list you just made, which area(s) of your life you would like to use this book to improve?—Choose one to three areas to focus on.

- Set an INTENTION for what you want in each of these areas- For example, if fitness is an area you want to improve in, you could set an intention that you will "consistently exercise for at least twenty minutes per day." If having some stress relief is a priority, set an intention to participate in twenty minutes of calm reading or meditation per day.

LEARN TO UN-LEARN

*"The first problem for all of us, men and women, is not to
learn, but to unlearn."*

—Gloria Steinem

You were born with passions. As a young child, you did a lot of
things you might not be doing now as an adult. You sang. You
danced. You colored hippopotamuses yellow with green polka-
dots just because you want to. You made your opinions known and
didn't care who was watching or judging.

Then as time rolled on, the "Nos" and "Stop thats" and "I don't
like when you do thats" slowly penetrated your self-view and you
changed. You learned to be quiet. You learned to conform. You
learned to be (too) careful. You learned to stifle and maybe even
to become fearful of your passions, or at least of sharing them with
others.

You may still dance, sing, and let your creative energies flow
when no one is watching you, but you've learned to keep it to yourself. You question yourself and hold yourself back

You may color from time-to-time, but the hippos are more of
a natural grey tone, and the whimsical is much less pronounced so
that you "fit in" and feel accepted.

You were not born with an inferiority complex. By all logic,
those early years in your life are when you should've felt inferior.
You were tiny. You cried a lot. You needed help when you pooped.

You couldn't feed yourself, and you always had a constant trail of snot running down your face. Assistance was needed in pretty much every single thing you did. Life could have been a mound of humility and insecurity for you. But funny enough, it was the opposite: you were completely comfortable and confident in your abilities. You weren't even factoring in what others may believe about you. You didn't feel inferior in any way.

If you need proof of this, go observe a toddler for a short while. Or better yet, just ask him to dress himself, and then say "hello" to the Batman cape, Ninja Turtle t-shirt, cowboy boots, and Spider-Man underwear ensemble he picks out. As a child, curiosity and creativity are embedded into all of your thoughts and actions. It isn't until you are taught to believe you don't "measure up" that you start to doubt yourself and feel inferior.

Self-doubt is a learned mentality.

Maybe your parents told you that you weren't good enough. Maybe you were constantly compared to a sibling who was better at math or soccer or spelling. Maybe you scored lower on tests than you friends. Maybe you weren't picked first in kickball. Or, maybe you were. Maybe you were the best at something, at everything. Maybe you were so good you felt guilty about it, or lost friends because of it. Being on that end of the comparison spectrum is just as dangerous. At that end you learn to hide your gifts. You learn that your talents are not meant to share with others.

When I was in my middle school years, I was playing competitive soccer. I played defense, and although I had some skill, I took on much more of a "run through the player and get the ball" sort of role. I was a tough defender, but my offensive skills were put on the back burner.

We had a transfer player from Europe come and play for our team. To this day I remember overhearing the following conversation: "Soccer is so much different in the United States than it is in Europe. In Europe there are players like Fernando (name changed for posterity) who are just so skilled with the ball, and here we have players like Joel, who are really just defenders and can only pass sometimes." They didn't intend for it to be hurtful, but because of that comment, I never really tried during shooting drills, or juggling drills, etc. I "learned" what sort of player I was supposed to be and I lived up to it.

It wasn't until I switched teams my final year of high school and the coach put me in as a midfielder that I started showing my other skills again (I scored twice against my old team in that season).

Through the years, you've probably even discovered ways to support these "truths," by finding proof that you are less capable than others, or proof that you shouldn't demonstrate how incredibly capable you really are. You fell in line and started marching through life, forgetting about what you had hammering inside of you, that drumbeat you used to march to. You allowed it to get quieter, and quieter and quieter. Over time you were taught (again, by others or by yourself) that it was better to play it safe and keep those talents tucked away.

It is time to unlearn all the lies you have accepted as truth.

Unlearn
> to forget and stop doing (something, such as a habit) in a deliberate way because it is false or incorrect (Source: Merriam-Webster's Learner's Dictionary).

How do you unlearn what may have been planted in your mind so long ago? Some of those roots run unfathomably deep. One way is to start digging. Where did the weeds start growing? When did these roots become so strong? Look back and try to remember the lies and the fears from your past, so you can find the root cause of them. When you look at obstacles straight on, when you face them, you'll realize they tend to shrink and are much easier to deal with.

For example, maybe you have a belief that says, "I'm not good enough."

Close your eyes and imagine that root. Grab it and move it around in your hand, allowing all of the soil to fall away. Touch the root so you can examine it more closely.

"I'm not good enough."

Really? Is that really true? Says who? When was the last time you actually heard someone say that to you? Consider: What evidence do I have to truly support that claim? What evidence do I have to contradict it? Is this thought a truth or a momentary opinion that I just blindly accepted?

Get all analytical on that thought.

At first you may find answers to those questions and the root may seem more powerful; the lie validated. For example, "Back in 7th grade that one popular kid told me I wasn't cool enough to sit at his lunch table." Or maybe in high school someone singled you out of the group because they didn't think you had the dance-fighting chops to be in the Jets or the Sharks (I'm sure you've seen West Side Story). Those situations are hardly designations for your future reality.

When you examine these false-truths at a deeper level, you realize the roots are not that solid.

So keep asking, keep chipping away, and the more you ask, the more reasons you will come up with to pull that weed, and eradicate it from the roots. When you go through this process, your long-held beliefs will start to show the withering in their leaves, and sometimes, the hidden lies underneath become blatantly obvious.

The more you bring these potentially harmful ideas to light, the more you question and examine them, the more they will shrivel and lose their hold on you. Who you are now is vastly different than who you were when you learned these false-truths holding you back.

Don't believe me? Ever heard of Albert Einstein? Young Albert didn't speak until he was four years old and didn't read until age seven. He was labeled a "dunce" and was also expelled from school.

Einstein had every reason to let these labels hold him back. Instead, he became even more inquisitive about the world around him. He learned to read, won a Nobel Prize, and basically changed the way people look at the world (and inspired Bobbleheads to be made in his likeness).

Tom Landry (famous coach of the Dallas Cowboys) had the distinction of having one of the worst seasons on record (never winning a game all year) and winning five or fewer games the next four seasons. He needed to completely revamp his scheme. So he invented the now very popular "4-3" defense in order to improve. He changed his roster, his playbook, and his formations. He eventually won two Super Bowl rings, five NFC Championship victories, and held the record for the most career wins.

At any given moment (like right now!), you can start your re-education process. You may not be able to fully pull the weeds out with one tug, but by working on these lies, by scrutinizing them, you will create room for new beliefs to grow. You get to decide what to plant there. You are good enough. You are exactly the person for the complicated job of being you. You are whole. You are the only you there is, and it's time to stop hiding. The weeds have taken over for far too long.

Unlearn. Your mind is your garden. Start cultivating.

PURPOSELY POSITIVE EXERCISE: UNLEARNIN'

Grab your notebook and do the following:

1. Write down the false beliefs you have held onto in your life—make a list of all of them.

2. Replace these false beliefs with empowering ones (even if you don't believe them yet)—write these new beliefs down.

3. Consider: how can you convince yourself to un-learn these falsehoods, and, instead learn new and empowering thoughts to propel you to your future?—write some ideas down and take action on them.

NUDGES

"In your days, things like this happen to you... you get a tap, a nudge, a gentle shake, and life whispers to you, 'I know you're tired-but I don't want you to miss this."

—MARY ANNE RADMACHER

When you travel along your journey of self-discovery, you will notice what I like to call "nudges." As you are navigating your life with purpose and inspiration, you will experience little pushes or little reminders to move on, to turn left, or veer right. The irony here is these nudges actually help you remain centered.

For example, you may notice a certain song keeps playing whenever you're in your car...*listen* to the lyrics, they most likely hold a message you need to hear. Four people throughout the day may mention the same book (or you hear about it once but something inside "pops" at its mention)...*buy the book*. If a certain person from your past keeps coming up in conversation (externally or internally)... *reach out to them*. You may keep seeing the same word on billboards, in magazines, on tv, and this word feels important...*investigate*.

Inspiration has many tools at its disposal (and yes, I am referring to Inspiration as an entity. I know that's kinda weird, but for more on this view, read *Big Magic: Creative Living Beyond Fear* by Elizabeth Gilbert, absolutely awesome book). Be open to these nudges of inspiration. They are trying to push you down the right path (or pull you away from the wrong one) so you can be the best YOU possible.

When I was studying Kinesiology (Sports Medicine) in college, I took an internship at a Children's Hospital, in the Orthopedics Department. It was great. I "scrubbed-in" for surgeries, casted kiddos with broken bones, followed my mentor, Dr. Glancy, on rounds, and input notes and x-rays into the computer. At that point in my life, I was sure I wanted to become an Orthopedic Surgeon. O.K. so I wasn't really "sure." I really had no clue what I wanted to do, but I liked health care, and my mom worked at the Children's Hospital, so I had an "in" for their program, I figured this may be exactly what I should pursue. I knew I liked the sound of "Dr. Lindeman."

I was a few months from graduating and the "real world" was looming right around the scary corner. I needed to make a decision. And while the internship was great, it didn't "light me up" as much as I hoped it would.

At this same time in my life, I was experiencing the joy of migraines. I would have searing pain in my forehead and above my eyes. At times I had to pull the car over to the side of the road, lest I create a demolition derby on I-25. When a migraine hit hard, I would succumb to napping away the day and hoping it would be gone when I woke up. Dr. Glancy sent me to a neurologist. I had MRIs and CT scans done, and (thankfully) I didn't have any strange growth in my brain. I was prescribed medicines that helped take some of the pain away, but the migraines were still happening.

In the midst of all this, we had a couple of speakers come to one of my classes at UNC (no, not the college with the amazing basketball team; I went to The University of Northern Colorado) from Cleveland Chiropractic College. I had no desire to listen to what they had to say. Except I had missed many of these classes already (in my defense, there was a gorgeous lawn right outside and we had a portable volleyball net), and was in jeopardy of getting a lower grade due to said absences. So I stayed and listened. They spoke about their field, how they were learning about Neurology, Biology, Biochemistry, Radiology, Physiology, and lots of other "ologys." They talked about how the Nervous System was the master controller of the entire body and coordinates every muscle, cell and tissue. They discussed how, as chiropractors, they help so many people with their health and wellness, and they didn't need to deal with surgery or handle any blood or bodily fluids. It all made a lot of sense to me and I was intrigued. I took it as a gentle nudge to learn more about Chiropractic.

I took the offer to fly out to Kansas City to investigate the school (and its surroundings). My wife (well, fiancé at the time) came with me and we explored the city a bit, toured the school and decided that this was what I should do. So I enrolled. In fact, Sheri and I graduated from UNC, got married, went on an amazing honeymoon to Maui, and moved to Kansas City, MO all in the span of a month.

During my time at Cleveland Chiropractic College, I enjoyed the material so much, I graduated Magne Cum Laude with a 3.85 GPA, won the Clinic Service Award and became fired up about my life. I have since loved this career more than I ever thought possible. I own my own clinic, I get to help more than one hundred people a day, I work twenty-four to twenty-six hours per week, and I get to experience miracles first-hand on an almost-daily basis. Life truly is awesome, and in reality, it's all because I followed some nudges along the way.

Nudges need to be followed, but they will not always be positive ones. You will also get "gut feelings" that tell you that you may be heading down the wrong path. You can find yourself in situations or even trains-of-thought that just don't feel right. You can get led astray in life, so don't beat yourself up too much. There is a lot going on in your life, it's only natural to get knocked off course sometimes. Remember, the failure isn't in the falling, it's in choosing to stay down. Listen to the nudges both to point you in the right direction and to pull you away from the wrong one.

Even with the most amazing intentions, you still need assistance from others, from your conscious thoughts and activities, from God and from the universe to help you stay on the right track.

PURPOSELY POSITIVE EXERCISE: NOTICE THE NUDGES

Grab your notebook (or use the "Notes" app on your phone) and do the following:

- For the next few weeks, be really observant of any nudges you may be getting—

- Do you keep hearing someone's name on the radio, in the book your reading, at school?

- Do you keep seeing the same car on the road?

- Does a friend from your past keep popping up in your head?

- Does a certain number appear all the time in your day-to-day?

- Write these nudges down.

- Research what they could mean—Sometimes it is obvious, if you keep seeing "mom" everywhere, you should probably give her a call.

- Other times it won't be as obvious, so have fun trying to figure out the clues and be happy in the knowledge that it will lead you somewhere that can help you in your life.

PIECE-FULL

"People spend their entire lives searching the world for the pieces that will make them whole, yet those pieces are only found within them."

—KEN POIROT

You are a conglomerate. All of your pieces are of vital importance because all together they make you whole. There are different sides of your personality, and you have used them all. For example, as a child, if you hadn't taken Ronda's lollipop (she had the strawberry, you had vanilla), and therefore hadn't seen her tears flow, you may not have learned the importance of kindness. If you never tried playing basketball at recess with the athletic kids, you might have never known that game just wasn't your "thing."

There isn't one word that can describe you, is there? The word(s) you choose may depend on the day, the month, the time, the angle of the sun, whether you're wearing an amazing suit, or going commando (honestly, I don't want to know). At times you're brimming with joy; you're enthusiastic; you're love. Other times you're feeling fear; you're sad; you're worried. You are a trusted friend to someone and the bane of existence to someone else. You may be proud and jealous. You may be so happy you got the new job, and so scared about the future. You are complex and cannot be summed up in a single word.

Of course you have faults, we all do. And the definition of faults I'm using here is not "problems," but rather, fracture lines or dividing lines. You are full of shards. You're a collection of pieces. Show me a person who you feel is 100%, totally "together," and I will show you that it's really like one of those old-time ads where the people are always smiling, but after the photographer snaps the picture, the family goes on fighting like cats and dogs.

It's the pieces that make you whole. In fact, it's the facets that make you shine. Don't wait to have a polished stone before you share your gifts with the world. The fractures create a mosaic: beautiful, jagged and full of character. That's you. That's me. The beauty is in the scars, the triumph over them, and the melding them into your soul. If you try to hide the blemishes or smooth them over, you hide yourself.

And if you truly wanted to hide, you wouldn't be reading this book. You want your soul to shine. You want your purpose to inspire others. You want to leave a legacy. Every single part of you is instrumental in that legacy. Improving parts of yourself is a very worthwhile endeavor. Hiding them or glossing over them, or using your pieces as an excuse to not bring your purpose to light, is a coward's lie...and you are NOT a coward.

Your character is deep, man (said in my best Tommy Chong voice). You have a piece that is all fire, all enthusiasm and all ready to change the world. Some motivational books will tell you to grab that piece, bring it to the front to focus on it, and leave the others in the deep recesses. I'm not going to do that. The pieces that make you cry, that make you immobile, that make you fear are just as important as the enthusiasm piece. It's a grave mistake to try to forget about all your other facets in the quest to find your spirit and let it thrive. All these other pieces are vital. These segments are there to serve, protect and help you. These parts need to be respected, revered and thanked.

You have emotions for every situation; you have every "color" known to science to decorate your life with, and I am not asking you to pick one (the shiniest one with sparkles) and throw out the rest. The truth of the matter is, in living your inspired life, you need to accept all your colors—the dismal and the shiny—so that you may pick the perfect one for each unique instance.

Decorate your world with every piece of you. Don't stifle. Don't hold back. In fact, you must attempt to find all of your pieces, name them, be grateful for them in order to be truly whole. One of the biggest lessons you'll learn when digging for your inspiration is that it's of utmost importance to accept who you are, in your entirety, to be vulnerable, and to have the courtesy to show your gifts, breaks and all.

You have a past. You have scars, wounds, and deformities (that are probably only visible to you). You also create blemishes inside your own head, as discussed in the last chapter. You have used these scars to imprison your soul, and you rationalize perfectly good reasons to keep this beauty locked up. Sometimes just the fear of digging up something you won't like or you fear others may judge you for keeps you from starting your soul-searching.

Remember history class? Every human being who is immortalized in textbooks had the same doubts and fears, but they decided to tell them to shut-the-hell-up and do what they were called to anyhow. If you attempt to only share yourself with the world when you're "whole," you will never have the opportunity to fully shine, and that's tragic for yourself and for all of those who would love to see your beautiful kaleidoscopic soul.

Embrace your facets and do as Pink Floyd suggests and "shine on, you crazy diamond."

PURPOSELY POSITIVE EXERCISE: WHO ARE YOU?

Grab your notebook and do the following:

- Think about WHO you are—really take some time for this one.

- Write down a list of all the things you feel are your "pieces"—consider things that have happened to you, experiences you've had, lessons you've learned.

- Consider your "labels"—are you a father? A sister? A brother? An athlete? A chef?

- Move on to characteristics—are you passionate? Are you lazy? Are you loving? Friendly? Introverted? Extroverted?

- Free-write on all of this for the next 10 minutes

- Go nuts. I bet once you get going, you will find you are an amazing conglomerate.

- Bask in the glory of all your pieces—take some time in reverence of all your amazing facets.

- Really look at your pieces—"hold" them up to the light, ooh-and-ahhh them. You have a lot of depth, you have a lot of titles and you do it so beautifully.

GO AWAY GUILT,
SHUN AWAY SHAME

"How blunt are all the arrows of thy quiver in comparison with those of guilt."

—ROBERT BLAIR

O ne might (incorrectly) think that in order to become more in-tune with your soul/your purpose, you will need to completely get rid of negative emotions. You think you'll need to call in the big guns to eradicate the "bad stuff," but that isn't the case.

Every single emotion you have is a gift. Each of these emotions plays a crucial role. I don't believe God created us with anything "useless," including emotions. I'm also not going to get into the "both sides of the same coin," the "yin/yang," or the "if a tree falls in a forest and no one is there, do the chipmunks still freak out" arguments here. "Negative" emotions have a place in life just as positive ones do. Negative feelings/emotions are there to warn you, to induce change, nudge you to incite action. Guilt is one such emotion.

Guilt is defined in the Merriam-Webster Dictionary as, "A bad feeling caused by knowing or thinking that you have done something bad or wrong." Seems pretty straight forward, right? Do something wrong, you should feel bad about it. Break into your parent's liquor cabinet with some friends when you should be attending high school classes, you should feel bad. If you drop-kicked a Muppet, you should feel bad (unless that was in the script, or if it was Animal. I bet he's the one Muppet who actually enjoys that sort of thing, he kind of has a masochistic thing going on). Stealing money from your dad's wallet so you can hang out with the "cool kids" at the mall, you should feel guilty. (I may or may not have just alluded to some instances from my own past to prove a point... yet rest assured, I've never met a Muppet).

When I was a teenager, I did plenty of things that necessitated guilt. I repeatedly ditched school to do absolutely nothing instead. I threw parties and wrecked my parent's furniture. I snuck out of my bedroom numerous times when I was grounded for throwing those parties. I damaged my first car, badly, when I attempted to drag race someone in front of the school (by the way, the car was a Hyundai Excel, not exactly drag racing material). I was arrested for a "failure to appear in court" warrant because I decided I didn't really need to attend my court date for an underage alcohol consumption ticket and I spent three days in jail.

I definitely went full bore into my teenage angst years, and I know I put my parents through some incredibly tough times. For years, I never worked through the guilt I had from these situations and I just let it grow and fester and morph into shame. And the shame poisoned my soul.

The problem isn't the guilt itself. It's there to throw up the flag that you need to stop what you're doing—you are not moving in the correct direction at that point in your life. You see, guilt is an enormously powerful catalyst to induce a change in your life. It becomes a huge problem if you either don't change, or if you wear that guilt like some kind of twisted badge of honor.

For me, the pain I caused my family, my friends and myself were the big slaps in the face that I NEEDED to change. Rather than listen, I kept taking those blows over and over again. At first glance, that doesn't make sense, but homo-sapiens have a strange ability to take things that hold us back, and we latch those puppies onto our ankles and weigh ourselves down to halt our growth, to slow ourselves, to smother our fires. Change only happened for me when I decided (many years later) to work through the shame and guilt, to release those weights from my life.

Guilt can be a fog. Many times you are actually being held captive by guilt, and you don't even know it. It has a way of seeping into your very being and proliferating there. And due to guilt's nature, you cannot see it clearly, you can't grab it, and you can't erase it. The only way to overcome guilt is to find out what caused that monster to begin with.

The original cause of your guilt is probably a valid one, and that root cause has never truly been confronted, investigated fully or dealt with, or you wouldn't still be feeling it. You are a (mostly) loving creature, so when you do something wrong that you KNOW is wrong, you feel guilt. If you don't do anything with that guilt, a far more sinister future awaits. It could be seconds, minutes or years later, but that guilt cloud will grow. As time goes on, the guilt becomes a bigger and bigger weight to your soul. The logical course of action is to go back to the cause of those negative feelings, the moment when the fog was first conceived, and un-do (or at least seek forgiveness for) the action(s).

Simple right? Simplicity isn't always reality.

The guilt cloud can exist for years/decades/centuries. It's not always easy to go back decades and apologize (I don't know about you, but I don't have a flux capacitor sitting in my garage, much less a DeLorean). Apologizing directly to the person you wronged, or think you've wronged, is not something you can check off your to-do list very easily. Or you may have already apologized and received forgiveness, but the guilt remains. That's not fair, but that's life. Some people hold themselves to a much higher standard than others. It seems very altruistic to think this way and, again, in the light vs. dark argument (that I said I wasn't going to go into... I may have fibbed), that would swing that balance to the light even more, right?

Well, if you hold yourself to a higher standard, doesn't that negate the golden rule (do unto others as you would have them do unto you)? If you punish yourself for things more harshly than you would someone else...you see where I am going here? I think many of us (and by "us" I mean I'm a card-carrying member of this club myself) have a tendency to hold onto guilt, or at least to know consciously, or subconsciously, that guilt has a hold on us, but we don't struggle too much to break free.

You almost feel comfort from the guilt. It becomes a security blanket, a "wubby," of sorts. It's serving its purpose—you use it as a reminder to try to be better, to keep yourself from getting too proud. *You may have won the Nobel Peace Prize, but remember when you broke your parent's favorite vase?* However, it also stifles your growth. When you continually cuddle up with your guilt, you will never realize that nothing you do in the present or the future will ever erase the past.

If you're willing to agree that guilt doesn't feel very good, can hold you back, and is a heavy load to carry, then it's certainly time to face the guilt and let go of the burden. If you can identify the guilt and what caused it, then you can seek forgiveness within and from others. Stop allowing the punishment to continue.

Punishment serves a purpose, but as anyone who has children knows, punishment alone doesn't teach. If your kid steals a cookie from the cookie jar and you punish him, he won't like it, but unless he knows WHY it's bad, he may steal again, and again, and again, and definitely when no one is looking. Children must be taught there are consequences but also learn from the experience for it to stick.

If you allow guilt to punish you forever and never look into what caused it, or you don't seek forgiveness, you won't be able to fully forgive yourself. If you CHOOSE to run a marathon with a refrigerator on your back, that's your choice (as a child I saw a race in a "Toughest Man Alive Competition" where a bunch of guys competed in a race doing just that... it didn't end well). But you can also choose to set the refrigerator down and finish the race without it.

There's another face of guilt. Some people are amazing at taking care of others, they give, they provide, and they receive a lot of joy in helping others. But (you saw that "but" coming, didn't you?) they have an incredibly hard time giving to themselves. They may feel guilty when they buy themselves something or when they take some time for themselves. They feel guilt when they give to themselves.

You may know someone like this. It may even be the person staring back at you when you brush your teeth in the morning. If not, you probably have someone close to you who feels this way (at least a little bit). This type of guilt is built upon a foundation of unworthiness. This guilt comes from self-deprecation and lashes out when you try to be compassionate with yourself. No problem in doing for others, just don't ever do unto yourself...I don't think that is how the saying is supposed to go.

There is no possible way you can provide joy for others unless you hold a reservoir of happiness inside yourself. You definitely receive joy in the service of others, no doubt there. It's just that, the person you spend the most time with is you. You must have compassion for yourself if you want a surplus to give to others.

The guilt you feel when doing things for yourself serves no one. In fact, it keeps you from serving to the best of your ability. It's a drain, and ultimately it limits your potential in helping others. Self-love is not selfish. In fact, it's absolutely necessary to be selfless. The fear of becoming narcissistic is just that, a fear (False Evidence Appearing Real). If you strive to improve *the* world, you need to improve *your own* world first, and a huge building block of that is getting rid of the guilt you feel when you look after the solidarity of your own foundation.

And here's the kicker: No one cares! Not a single person can see the guilt that is holding you back. And 99.9% of the time the person(s) you think you're carrying the guilt around for has long-ago forgotten, or at least moved on. They aren't carrying *your* fridge on *their* run through life. In order to harm someone, the other party has to allow it, in some part. They don't necessarily lay out the red carpet and ask you to hurt them, but they do play a role. That doesn't excuse you from your part, but it does serve as a reminder that it is a two-way street, and in allowing guilt to hold you back (regardless of the reason), it doesn't help them, you, your children, your neighbors, your pet salamanders or your Uncle Billy.

One must realize guilt is a very powerful and useful emotion when used to provoke change. So beg forgiveness, then forgive yourself so CHANGE will manifest. When you feel guilt for taking care of yourself, you should accept that as a signal to change.

When you allow guilt to hold you back, you are misappropriating its use. You are not using your gifts the way they should be used. The world is not improving to the extent it could be because you are muting your impact. You are not becoming the person you are destined to become. You're allowing the past to be an anchor, holding your back from a brighter future. In essence, you are giving the finger to your Creator. You are not living an inspired life, and you most certainly are not inspiring.

Guilt is a learned emotion, whose gritty surface makes you grasp tighter. After a while, guilt can become a suppressor, stopping you from loving fully, from following your heart, from being creative, from expanding, from growing, from living. Don't allow the scars of the past to inflict pain on your present and your future. Stop picking at those scabs just to see them bleed again. Stop "shoulding" yourself so much. Guilt, when used correctly, can push you toward new horizons. But when you let guilt morph into shame, you carry that weight around wherever you go. You bottle it up, instead of using it as a stimulus for change. You coddle the guilt and let it transform into something far more negative.

Carrying shame around allows you to think of all the things/feelings/actions you "should" do, but never allows any real change to occur. Shame is a much deeper feeling. Shame disconnects you from your higher self and dims your light. When you feel guilty for things you have done to others, or to yourself, and don't work to resolve the origin of those feelings, shame takes hold and becomes embedded in your life. Shame can become an addiction. In reality, shame is rooted in most well-known addictions. The emotions stirred from shame are strong. They may not be pleasurable, but they are addicting because of their strength. Trust me, I know.

I allowed the shame from my teenage years to fester for so long, addictions were created, relationships suffered, and my growth as a human being was smothered. And to be honest, for a long while

I actually enjoyed the power of shame. It gave me so many strong reasons to not try, to not attempt to be a better husband, father, brother, doctor, friend, and human being. It wasn't until I sought help (through the form of counseling, reading, and plain apologizing to my parents and siblings) that I began to feel free and capable of becoming the type of person I could become, the type of person that those around me deserved.

Look into your guilt, accept it (burying it just gives it a more solid foundation). Be grateful for the reminder to be better. Learn from the experience and then release yourself from its grasp. You may never be totally free from guilt, but you can lighten that load and move forward into growth.

Shame may have been a scapegoat in your life, but you need to drop that blanket to forge a more purposeful life. Today, you can decide to move forward, to grow, to realize that you deserve a better future.

PURPOSELY POSITIVE EXERCISE: GARBAGE YOUR GUILT

Grab your notebook and do the following:

- Ask yourself: Is there anything from your past that still has its claws in you?—make a list of anyone/anything that stands out to you.

- Take some time to think about a person, place or thing that you feel guilty about—if you can't think of any, then great-you get a hall pass during this exercise. Go ahead and move on to the next chapter, sing some Karaoke or spend the next ten minutes patting yourself on the back. Otherwise:

- Describe the event. Why do you feel guilty? Delve deep. Lay out the situation in all its atrocity in your notebook. You may even find it beneficial to draw a picture of the situation, or draw what your guilt feels like. It's O.K. if you shed a tear or four.

- Think about what you can you do to "right the wrong"— if you're honest with yourself, you've been going over the situation a thousand times in your head (that's why it still has weight). So what can you do to reduce this guilt's hold on you? You have options. You don't need to allow this feeling to hold you back.

- Write down everything you can think of that you can do to "right the wrong," and then pick something from the list and go do it. Repeat as necessary until the guilt has released its hold.

DROP ANCHOR...AND SET SAIL

"To reach a port we must sail, sometimes with the wind, and sometimes against it. But we must not drift or lie at anchor."

—OLIVER WENDELL HOLMES, SR.

After reading the last chapter, I'm sure you realize that guilt can hold you back from living a truly amazing life. But guilt is only one of those weights that holds you down. There are many anchors that you carry on a day-to-day basis. You need to drop all of those anchors, cut the proverbial cord and then set sail onto newer, better horizons.

But, where do these anchors come from? Nature or Nurture?

I'm sure you've heard that argument before. Here's a quick run-down: there's one school of thought that says who you are is primarily due to the nature of your life. You are a combination of genes, genotypes, xenotypes and phenotypes. Who you are is simply written in your DNA.

The nurture end of the spectrum says that when you are born you're basically a "blank slate," a void, a vacuum, and by your interactions with your parents and your environments, who you are takes shape.

Nature says who you are is, in essence, "preordained." Nurture says who you are is created as you go through life.

There is definitely a lot of in-between stances as well and I, myself, subscribe to a "bit of each" philosophy. I do believe that a lot of our issues/hurdles/challenges/messed-up-ness come from our parents and siblings. I was the youngest in my family, so I know the havoc siblings can bring (and the joy, there is a lot of that also—just in case any of them are reading this book). I also believe that a lot of our troubles/strife/wack-a-doodle-weirdness comes from our very own selves. You take some of what our nature gave you, mix it with how you choose to react to situations in life, and a personality is made (and remade over and over again). The latest research supports this stance as well. A study published in *Nature Genetics*[1] revealed that roughly 49% of human traits and diseases in twins were due to genetics and about 51% were due to environmental factors. That's pretty close to a 50/50 split in the realm of research.

The problem here is that you can't just point to one cause as the root of all issues, and I'm sure you realize, we ALL have issues. It would be so liberating to be able to say, "All the troubles in my life are due to the way cousin Matilda picked on me as a child." Or to say, "It's because I have been genetically encoded to forgo my parent's dreams of me leaving the house for the first time in eight months." You can say those things, but also know that those statements smell (and taste) like bull-pucky, and you know the importance of fresh-breath.

Even more important is the fact that, regardless of where these gigantic weights you carry around come from, is that it's up to you and you alone to drop them and move more nimbly toward your passion-filled future. If you can stop throwing stones with your feet firmly planted in the Nature or Nurture (or variations in-between) side of the battlefield, you can stop to realize no matter where you are, the stones keep coming. There will always be a lifetime supply

---

1. Polderman TJ, Benyamin B, de Leeuw CA, Sullivan PF, van Bochoven A, Visscher PM, Posthuma D: "Meta-analysis of the heritability of human traits based on fifty years of twin studies." *Nature Genetics volume 47.7 (2015) 702–709.*

of heavy things to hold you back. But only if you continue to allow them to.

These encumbrances come in many shapes and sizes. One of the largest, no doubt, is guilt, as discussed earlier. Forgiveness is the key to letting this anchor loose. You also may be carrying around things that you need to forgive others for. Maybe you were hurt in the past, maybe even severely crushed. It isn't always easy to forgive those who injured you. However, if you walk around with these wounds and never let fibrosis do its job to form a scar, you will never heal. Forgiveness is more about giving a gift to yourself rather than those who hurt you anyway.

This practice takes some serious dedication, and meditation is a great tool to help you practice forgiveness. Just picture the person in your mind, imagine yourself saying that you forgive him or her.

If meditation isn't your thing, write a letter to the offending party (and send or don't send it, that's not truly the point). Whatever you decide to do, forgiveness is a process that we all need to go through. Until you forgive others, you carry a large burden with you wherever you go.

Take inventory of your weights. Look to see where they came from, because that is part of the process of releasing them. To some extent, it doesn't matter what created the cancer, for example, your job is simply to begin treatment.

So take inventory of what weighs on you. Seriously. Sit in some quiet time with a pen and a paper, or a giant notebook, if needed. Write down what you feel is keeping your butt firmly in place. Fear? Inadequacy? Comparison? Guilt? Those shoes you insist on wearing? Write it all down.

YOU need to figure out YOUR anchors, bring them to light, and get to work on dropping them from your ship.

I also don't want you to think that this is a one-time thing. You won't face a large demon from your past, bring it to light, and cut it free forever on the first try. Many of your anchors will never truly be left behind. You will just get better and better and better at facing them each time they come up, which will soften the ramifications with each uninvited visit.

Sometimes, letting go of your anchors will be harder than you think. Sometimes you've had these anchors on your shoulders for such a long time they have become comforting companions. (You may hate the things that damn parrot says, but you still want to lug him around with you on sailing excursions.) Change is always uncomfortable, even when you are shedding negative things from your life. So be prepared. Know that removing things from your life is not going to be easy, and that may be due to your perceived "need" for the negativity (as I talked about in the intro of this book). There is nothing wrong with this. Just get to work on finding what's holding you back so you can move on to the all-important work of shedding the excess weight and setting sail.

PURPOSELY POSITIVE EXERCISE: ANCHORS AWEIGH!

Grab your notebook and do the following:

- Name your anchors—start small if you have to, but work up to the big ones. Think about the heavy ones that you know you're carrying with you every morning along with your briefcase/purse after you finish your coffee.

- Answer the following questions: what are you afraid of?

- What stops you from moving forward in your life?

- Do the "Lighten the load" visualization—a counselor (Micheal Perry) had me go through a great exercise concerning this. It will help you see that you can release the things that are holding you back, and will soon find that a happier, more productive life exists right behind them.

  ○ Once you write out all your anchors, take some time to lay back and close your eyes. Imagine yourself lying in a field, under a cloudy sky.

- ○ Picture the words you've written in the clouds overhead. Really focus on them.

- ○ Realize that the clouds aren't all that thick.

- ○ Notice the sunlight that wants to burst through behind them.

- ○ Concentrate on bursting these clouds.

- ○ Picture them dissolving away, letting the warm light to shine through.

- ○ Do this with each anchor one-by-one.

- Drop the weights, set sail—repeat this exercise as needed.

IN-PROVE

"We improve ourselves by victories over ourselves. There must be contest and we must win."

–Edward Gibbon

I know you have within you a desire to improve. To make your life and the lives of your loved ones better. To make the world a better place. (Otherwise you wouldn't be reading this book.) I want every human on the planet to do their damnedest to do those very things. Strive to leave the world a better place than you found it. But first things first: in order to improve the outside, it's certain that you must start on the inside. The seed you have within you to enhance the world is partially planted there to prove to yourself that you are worthy of such a task.

Statistics abound in the realm of low self-esteem, and they ain't pretty. Seventy eight percent of women age seventeen are "unhappy with their bodies."[1] In another study, researchers found seven out of ten girls feel they do not measure up in some way, including their looks, their schoolwork or other achievements.[2] Men aren't

---

1. *Teen Health and the Media https://depts.washington.edu/thmedia/ view.cgi?page=fastfacts&section=bodyimage*
2. Shapiro, Hannah. "Dove's Campaign for Real Beauty boosts girls' self-esteem for Back to School." Examiner.com. Accessed March 3, 2014. *http://www.examiner.com/article/dove-s-campaign-for-real-beauty-boosts-girls-self-esteem-for-back-to-school.*

exempt from this either. Studies have shown that male and females share in the body image dissatisfaction.[3]

Self-esteem is not tied exclusively to body image, however. Your self-worth is many times improperly connected to your accomplishments or your perceived successes, or lack-there-of. In 1978, clinical Psychologists Pauline R. Clance and Suzanne A. Imes coined the term/diagnosis "Imposter Syndrome" to describe the feelings people have when they achieve renowned success, but inside feel unworthy of their accolades/growth. They feel that at any time they will be called out, exposed as a fraud or an imposter. Psychological research in the 1980s found that 70% of people have fit into this mold at one point or another.[4] Odds are, you have felt this way too. If so, you're in good company: Maya Angelou, Tom Hanks, Emma Watson and Michelle Pfeiffer have all stated they felt this way at some point in their careers.

Inadequacy about your body, low self-esteem hindering you from improving your life, and if/when you do improve, thoughts that you are an imposter... it's no wonder you feel frozen.

When we lived in Kansas City, MO, my (heart-stoppingly) beautiful wife, Sheri, and I were on a swift fifteen mile jog through the country. It was a beautiful spring day, birds were singing, bees buzzing and all of that, when we stopped at an intersection. O.K., so we were really just taking a quick jog alongside of Holmes Avenue to get some necessities from the grocery store, but it was beautiful nonetheless.

Something was "off" at the intersection. Literally off. The stoplight (or at least the power box that controlled the stoplight) was off and sitting in the middle of the street, and the stoplight resembled a certain tower in Italy.

My highly intellectual mind went to work right away. I said to my wife, "Huh, that's weird, babe. I think there's an ATM machine in the middle of the road. You can't just grab those things out of

3. McCabe M, Ricciardelli L. "Body Image Dissatisfaction Among Males Across the Lifespan" *Journal of Psychosomatic Research* 56.6 (2004): 675-685.
4. Sakulku, Jaruwan and Alexander, James. "The Imposter Phenomenon." *International Journal of Behavioral Science* 6.2 (2011): 75-97

the ground. The guy who did that must've been huge!" My wife
noticed the stoplight and deduced (she has always loved detective
novels and TV shows) there had been an accident. There was, of
course, some other evidence. To our left, a car, or rather, the back
end of a car, was sticking out of the front of the local sandwich
shop. It seemed someone had fallen asleep at the wheel, ran into
the stoplight, hit the power box off, careened into the parking lot
and ran smack into the restaurant. Luckily, no one was sitting in
the booths at the front. We moved toward the scene and noticed
at least ten people with their phones out. Obviously, someone had
called 9-1-1 for help, right?

Well, it seems getting pictures of the incident to post on social
media was more important than that. We asked one of the workers
at the restaurant if anyone was injured. He told us he didn't think
so, then proceeded to drop his apron and said he was going home,
because he'd had "enough of this crappy day." No one had even spo-
ken to the woman who'd been driving the vehicle.

My wife immediately told one of the amateur YouTube film-
makers to call 9-1-1 (they did) and we found the driver of the car.
She had a huge welt on her head, and you don't need to be a Chiropractor (shameless plug) to know that she probably had some in-
juries besides what we could see. We calmed her down, spoke to the
person she was trying to talk to on the phone and had one of the
sandwich shop workers who didn't go home bring out some ice and
a first aid kit. Soon, an ambulance came, we gave our statements
to discuss what we saw/didn't see, and the driver was taken to the
hospital.

What does this situation have to do with anything else we have
been discussing, besides the fact it shows that life can be a bit cray-
cray? It demonstrates one huge point. Of all the people who saw
this thing unfold, no one called 9-1-1, and no one checked on the
lady involved in the accident. Why? Some were too excited to post
this thing on their Facebook page or send it to a friend, but others
were paralyzed with fear. They were afraid to check on the driver.
They may have talked themselves into the "someone else probably
called" and "someone else is probably going to check on her" lies,

but in reality, they probably had a fear of not being good enough at explaining it, and at taking responsibility to help. They were afraid to take charge. They were afraid they weren't adequate enough to help. The injured party would be better off letting anyone else take charge (but no one does).

Sounds kinda crazy, right? The truth is (if you have ever taken any CPR or Basic Life Support classes you already know this), a lot of people won't step in to help because they think someone else who is "more trained" or "more knowledgeable" can step in and do it, and so most people do nothing. Studies show that only about 15% to 30% of people would actually administer CPR[5] to someone who needed it. Most people think they aren't the "right ones for the job."

This all leads up to a very important point: you are the ONLY one who is trained and knowledgeable enough about YOU and YOUR purpose to share it with others. You are the only person trained to conduct inspirational CPR on your life. You can decide to allow all situations and episodes of growth in your life to happen by chance and just go through the day-to-day by watching things unfold, or you can "take off your apron" and just go home/give up because you aren't "right for" the very important job of being your (true) self.

There is one other option: you can decide that you are the ideal person to change your life and you can conquer your fear of inadequacy and forge your glorious life for the betterment of all.

The fear you have of inadequacy has no basis. The flip-side of inspiration is fear, and fear keeps you stuck right where you are. I'm not bad-mouthing fear here. Fear (like all emotions) is vitally important to your survival. If you didn't have fear, plain and simple... you'd be fertilizer by now. A healthy fear of picking a fight with a honey badger is a good thing. Don't lose that survival fear. The key is knowing the difference between that and the nonsense voices that fear puts into your head. Fear is about withdrawing (and with good reason), but it should never lead you.

---

5. "Top 5 Reasons to Get CPR Training" *Bifd.org, http://www.bifd.org/pdfs/5%20Reasons%20to%20Learn%20CPR.pdf*

During this journey into your soul, into finding your inspiration in order to cultivate and share it, you need to understand fear will attempt to hold you back at every turn. Your job isn't necessarily to tell it to shut up, but to acknowledge your fears and thoughts of inadequacy, and then to push on anyway. Let fear have its words. Let fear talk trash. Let fear tell you that you aren't good enough. Let fear poke fun, point out the gigantic zit on your forehead (we've all had that one, right?). By all means let fear have its voice.

But then get to work proving your fear wrong. Because, similar to the story I just told you, the person with the head injury (all those people you can help by sharing your amazing self and your passion) deserves it. Don't allow yourself to sit by and let fear win your soul. We ALL deserve for you to overcome those fears, because you have something that the world needs.

Now don't make the mistake of thinking in order to be valuable you need to do something massive, like eradicate the common cold, or eliminate world hunger (yet if you can do those things, then please do them). We all have different purposes, and whatever your purpose is, the rest of us need you to share it. We can't all be action heroes or professional athletes, or inventors or musicians or some mixture of all the above. You may not be called to run into a burning building to save a zillion fluffy puppies, win a Pulitzer Prize for literature, or to invent the most delicious ice cream flavor ever (just think about that, there are probably hundreds of ice cream flavors that haven't even been created yet! Life is amazing). You can improve the world simply by letting yourself shine, regardless of the "hat" you end up wearing.

You do not need to be a rescuer, or a shining knight, but you do need to be a soul-surgeon, and the only soul you can ever operate on is your own. Prep for surgery.

In order to truly live your life the way you were destined to, you need to go inside yourself. You need to discover what lies there. To overcome your hindrances, you need to be willing to learn about yourself. You need to delve deeper into why you truly don't feel you are worthy of a better life. Bring those ideas into the light and watch them dissolve away. You must find out exactly who you are right now. There is a 0% chance that you can be an imposter in your own skin. You are the ONLY one cut out for the astonishing job of being you. Once you step into being all that you are, you will realize that you can make the choice to let your self-worth skyrocket. You get to decide.

As you dig deeper into your soul, to find that fire of inspiration, you need to have your ears open and listen to your fears, and then get grinding to PROVE those voices wrong.

PURPOSELY POSITIVE EXERCISE: INTERNAL INTERVIEW (A LA BUDDY THE ELF)

The purpose of this exercise is to get to know yourself on a deeper level so you know what you're working with on your journey.

Grab your notebook and pretend "Buddy" (Will Ferrell's character in the movie, *Elf*) is following you down the street, bombarding you with questions and you have no choice but to answer them all:

- What is your #1 favorite food?

- What is your favorite beverage?

- What is the one thing you think you could do for the rest of your life?

- What is your biggest dream right now?

- Who is your best friend?

- Who do you admire most?

- What has been your favorite place you've ever visited?

- Where would you go tomorrow if money and time were no object?

- What's your favorite sport?

- What's your favorite movie?

- What is your favorite smell?

- What is your favorite vegetable, favorite fruit?

- What are you most afraid of (spiders, clowns, public speaking, success, etc.)?

- What do you dread doing every week?

- What is your least favorite part of the day?

- What actor can you not stand (hopefully not Will Ferrell)?

VOICES

"Your subconscious is always listening to and believing what you repeatedly say about yourself. So try not to become your own enemy of progress."

—EDMOND MBIAKA

"If you heard someone talking to your spouse the way that you talk to yourself, you'd kick their ass!"

—BRENT HENDON D.C.

You have a voice (probably more than one) in your head. And research has actually shown that by talking to yourself, you can actually improve your situation in life. In a study published in *The Quarterly Journal of Experimental Psychology* ('cause, you know, we all read *that* journal...at least quarterly), objects were hidden around a room and subjects were asked to find a specific one. Some subjects were told to repeat the word of the object they were looking for over and over "phone, phone, phone." The others were asked to search silently. Across the board, those who talked to themselves found the objects faster.[1] So there is power in using your voice. Which is great... except the studies also show your in-

---

1. Lupyan Gary, Swingly, Daniel "Self Directed Speech Affects Visual Search Performance." *The Quarterly Journal of Experimental Psychology* 65.6 (2012): 1068-1085.

ternal dialogue, on average, throughout the day tends to be negative. Your inner voice points out problems, inadequacies, worries, fears, pain, etc. You don't usually sit around telling yourself to marvel at the awesomeness of yourself, you job, your family, your food, your luck. Your mind has been primarily trained to point out problems. That stinks. However, maybe this is evolutionary?

When you were a cave-boy or cave-girl (seems like a long time ago, doesn't it? You rocked that leopard skin onesie!), you probably needed to be on the lookout for the negative. Predators were trying to eat you pretty consistently—watch out for that Tyrannosaurus Rex. Survival was kind of important to you. It makes sense that your mind was trained to search for problems then.

In the modern era, you need not be on the lookout for Saber-toothed tigers anymore, yet the roots of those voices are still there, and they are still Debbie-Downers. I have not read of a dinosaur attack in the Sunday newspaper in quite some time (actually, I really only like the Sunday paper for the ads and the comics anyway), but the voices that were initially put inside your head for protection still rage on.

You are constantly giving yourself lectures based on fear. In everyday social situations, the threat of being mauled by various gigantic flesh-eating animals is pretty much gone, but the fangs still persist. You hold yourself to some incredibly high "standards." You compare yourself to what the voices say you should look like, dress like, feel like. You battle your mirror and wage wars within your soul.

"*I'll never be good enough." "I'm too fat." "They won't like me." "I'll never get that job/promotion/girl/boy/house/car.*" The volleys keep coming and coming. And there is almost never any return-fire. It's really amazing you're still standing, considering the barrage of word-bullets that are self inflicted upon you daily.

As an experiment, take a pen and pad around with you throughout the day (or use the "Notes" app on your phone), and jot down any negative self-talk/thoughts you notice. I'm confident by the time your day is done, you'll have created prose so prolific even Emerson would be proud (of the quantity, not the quality).

You need to stop the bleeding. You need to arm your-self...against yourself. Be prepared to fight back when the villain-voice strikes. Sometimes you will see the attack coming. Getting out of the shower, combing your hair, looking at magazines with all the "beautiful" people, those are pretty predictable battle zones. So you can prepare for them by coaching and having an internal dialog with yourself, rather than listening to what these voices are saying. You can choose to fire the first shot.

"I am looking forward to exercising and eating healthier"

"I love the way I look when I smile."

"I am proud of who I am today."

"I am grateful for _____."

Filling your bandoliers with positive ammunition helps limit these frontal attacks. One of the best ways to stock up your armory with positivity is to use affirmations. Just start a routine of begin-ning—and while you're at it, ending—each day with some self-love. Tell yourself what you need to hear. Studies have shown that positive affirmations can increase grades in school-aged children, increase problem-solving in adults, and reduce stress in everyone. Further research shows that even more powerful than self-affir-mations, is a self-question. Rather than just saying, "I'm going to do awesome at the presentation today," it's even more powerful to bring a question into the mix. For example, "What does my audi-ence want to hear? I will do great today because I can deliver that."

Or, instead of, "I'm not good enough for this position," you could ask: "What attributes do I have that allow me to be perfect for this job right now?"

The good thing about asking the question is it begs for an an-swer. When you start that dialogue, you are more apt to uncover layers and solutions to the negativity. Your brain is wired to find answers to questions. So don't accept the self-defeating words as a proclamation. Challenge them with a question and find an answer.

If you implement positive self-talk into your daily life, the negative voices can be fought and beaten.

Sometimes the negative talk isn't as predictable. Sometimes negative self-talk is a shadowy ninja, creeping in through the fog to strike when you least expect it. In these instances, the best thing to do is to parry (aka mount a counter-strike).

For example, at the park you might be thinking: "Wow he really has his stuff together, I'll never be THAT good of a father." The parry would be: "But I know my kids love me, so I must be doing something right."

Or if you're sitting at a red light and a guy in an Italian sports car pulls up next to you, for example, you might think: "I will never be able to afford a car like that; I'll probably never be that cool." The parry would be: "I have a car, a home, a job, and I've got a lot of life to live. Who knows what will happen? And besides, I know quite a few people who think I'm 'cooler than a polar bear's toenails' (thank you for that quote Outkast). So I'm doing pretty great."

One way I have implemented this into my daily life involves some pretty hi-tech equipment: a mirror and a dry erase marker. I think of something positive I need to hear, and then I write it on the top of my bathroom mirror. When I'm brushing my teeth, the phrase is there. When I'm flossing, the phrase is there. When I take the two minutes to style my hair, the phrase is there. I do the same thing for my wife and my children. I leave them notes about how amazing they are on a consistent basis, so that when they're doing whatever it is they do in front of the mirror (I don't want to know), they will see these phrases and it will help set the stage for their day. Light (aka positivity) travels at 670,616,629 miles per hour (crazy, right?). So writing these messages out and then reading them to yourself sends a boost of positivity into your cerebral cortex at lightning speed.

Sound travels pretty dang fast too. The speed of sound is somewhere around 767 miles per hour, not as fast as light, but definitely a tiny bit faster than I can race-walk. You can combat the negativity by speaking some self-love into your daily life as well. Ask the right questions and work on monitoring the voices that control the conversations in your mind. And make no mistake, you may not consciously be spouting negativity: "Hey, what can you do to make me feel like crap today?" But when you're passive to it and not proactive about it, you're still allowing those voices to run the roost.

It will take some work for you to get into fighting shape. The good news is you get to practice multiple times per day. In fact, there will be no shortage of practice opportunities, and this will definitely help you get better. Arm yourself with positivity each day, and you can be like Rocky, running up the steps to the Philadelphia Museum of Art while carrying a bad-ass Katana, ready to swing, parry, and ninja-strike the negativity back to the shadows from whence it came! (I've always wanted to use that phrase.)

PURPOSELY POSITIVE EXERCISE: NOTICE ALL THE THINGS YOU TELL YOURSELF.

The "Negative Voices" exercise is good on multiple fronts: it's great to notice your thoughts (more on that later), and you will most likely be astounded at all the negativity you have (against inanimate objects and against yourself).

To get started, do the following:

- Carry a pen and a notebook with you all day (or use the "Notes" app on your phone), and when you think a negative thought, jot it down. Do this for a couple days (or at least until you notice how often you let negativity have a voice. You may need a lot of paper).

- Bad thought about the weather? Write it down.

- Thinking about how crappy it is you have a meeting today? Put it down on paper.

SYNAPTOGENIC NEUROPLASTICITY

"People laugh at me because I use big words, but if you have big ideas you have to use big words to express them, haven't you?"

—LUCY MAUD MONTGOMERY

"I like big words and I cannot lie."

—SOME ENGLISH MAJOR IN COLLEGE TRYING TO BE FUNNY BY MISQUOTING SIR MIX-A-LOT

S ynaptogenic Neuroplasticity, now there's a couple of words that would surely win you any Boggle contest. Before you roll your eyes and skip ahead to the next chapter, let's delve into this phrase just a bit more, shall we?

Synaptogenic: of or pertaining to synaptogenesis

O.K., we are going to have to go a bit deeper with that definition...

SYNAPTOGENESIS
  the formation of synapses (communication areas/links) between neurons and axons in the body.

So synaptogenesis is the formation of new communication areas between nerves. Got it?

NEUROPLASTICITY

The brain's ability to reorganize itself by forming new neural connections throughout life. Neuroplasticity allows the neurons (nerve cells) in the brain to compensate for injury and disease and to adjust its activities in response to new situations or to changes in its environment.

It was thought for many years that the human brain had a finite amount of cells and that you "get what you get" and no new cells can be formed or rearranged. As it turns out, that is simply bogus. Throughout your life, certain areas of your brain are able to create new nerve cells and rearrange pathways in order to adapt to what's going on. Now, I think this is awesome (Since I'm a Chiropractor, nerves are pretty much my 'thing,' so I may be biased). I'm pretty sure, given you're reading this book, you are also going to be thrilled for this discovery.

Your "flaws," your "faults," your "skills," have helped create pathways in your brain, and then these pathways have been reinforced, multiplied, reduced, etc., in order to make it easier for you to be who you are. Throughout your life, you've learned (via others and yourself) who you should be, how you should act, what you should do. When you acted on these "shoulds," you actually created communication centers in your brain, making it less cumbersome for you to do/be/have those qualities.

Think of riding a bike. I'm willing to bet you were not a BMX trick riding champ the first day you hopped on your trusty tricycle. You fell, scraped your knee, cried a bit, got some ice cream out of the whole deal, and maybe even an awesome Band-Aid with a Transformer, Voltron or Care Bear on it. Then you got back up and attempted to cruise down your driveway again and again until you figured it out. The more you tried to ride that bike, the better you became at it until eventually it was second nature (and all the neighborhood girls whistled and hooped and hollered at your bike-riding prowess). Riding a bike actually became a habit. You don't have to consciously think about the steps to ride anymore.

If riding a bike isn't your thing, the same scenario can be applied to brushing your teeth (minus the falling, scraping your knee and the girls whistling). At first you had to be taught how to brush. I'm willing to bet when you brush your teeth everyday, you don't have to sit and think about how to do each and every step. It's almost a "mindless" activity at this point. You have synatogenified some serious neuroplasticity in the realm of teeth-brushing! (You should receive some sort of medal, don't you think?)

These same concepts can be applied to any series of thoughts or actions you have in your daily life. Think, do, say or act something enough times and new pathways form in your nervous system, making it easier to think, do, say or act those things again. Tying your shoes, going to the bathroom, brewing your coffee, being unhappy, feeling like you aren't doing enough, fear, worry, all of these things become habitual and reinforced the more you do (and think) them. When you focus on your fear, your worry, your low self-esteem, you are ingraining it into yourself, not just in the mental sense, but in the physical sense as well. You're removing the barriers to feeling crappy about it... that kinda sucks to know, doesn't it?

When you have thoughts, your magnificent brain will attach a hormone/chemical response to that thought. By virtue of your amazeballs brain, this cause-effect relationship becomes solidified the more you have that same thought. It becomes easier and easier for the chemical to be released with the aforementioned thought. When you create bad habits, those habits are continually reinforced until you work to break them. And yes, the negative thoughts are largely due to habits you've created. You've been taught and/or taught yourself to think a certain way, to view the world through a certain lens, to act in a specific way, and therefore to secrete certain hormones and chemicals into your bloodstream.

If you can accept the fact that things need to change (even a little bit), you are going to have to accept that you need to create new habits. You need to form new synapses that lead you down the road(s) you want to travel. Notice the cycles you have created. Pay attention to the negativity as it rears its head. Understand that the bad habits you've created are by your own doing, and by virtue of the life you have lived so far. Those habits have formed strong connections in your brain that now produce effects that are contrary to what you actually want to think, feel and achieve.

The good news is, because your brain and nervous system are amazing, you can reverse that trend. For example, if you're overweight and you start to exercise, eat right, and create habits out of doing so, you will lose weight. I'm sure there's no argument there. If you start working on yourself, increasing your self-worth, increasing your inspiration, giving more to others; if you start being more compassionate, more resourceful, more grateful, more motivated, happier and more at ease, you will remove barriers to feeling this way too. When you work on yourself in this regard, you make it easier to go down the right path in life.

So how do you go about getting rid of bad habits? You need to replace them with good ones. It isn't possible to simply erase things you no longer want to do, you must switch them out with better ones. And there is a process you can do to achieve this.

First things first: schedule time to take part in the new habit. Don't expect the time to magically appear. Research shows that when you plan an activity, especially at a certain time in your day, the world will bend to allow you to fit that activity or thought process in. If you want to go to the gym, for example, write it out in your journal or add it to your Google calendar.

Next: start with little steps. You cannot immediately create a new habit of going to the gym everyday if the last time you went was fifteen years ago when you were forced to in high school. Start by going for one day, then celebrate that victory (more on that in the coming chapters). Positive reinforcement goes a long way in habit creation (be it a habit of exercise, meditation, eating healthier, thinking positively, using a Kleenex to wipe your nose rather than your sweatshirt, etc.).

Next: find someone to help you in this aim. Changing habits is so much easier if you have a coach or friend to keep you accountable and to help you celebrate your steps in the process.

And finally: make sure you have a list of the benefits of creating this new and keep it handy. This will help you keep the positive reasons you're making this change top-of-mind.

Repeat these steps over and over, and stick with it for at least a few months (some studies show a habit forms in twenty-one days, others say much longer) and your glorious new habits will eventually achieve solidarity. These same processes can be applied to creating any kind of new habits, including changing the way you think, meditation, reading, stopping negative self-talk, etc. Just go through the same steps with consistency, and then look back in awe at your neuroplasticity mastery.

You can forge your future by creating new habits. It's possible, by virtue of practice and physiology, to move from the negative slant of life toward a positive one. You can reverse the negative spiral and climb to the summit. You can create the life you want to live. You can *train* yourself, quite literally, to move into being the person you want to become.

PURPOSELY POSITIVE EXERCISE: HABITUAL BREAKDOWN

Grab your notebook and do the following:

- Think of a mundane task—something you do every single day involving multiple steps that you probably don't even think about anymore. For example, riding your bike, brushing your teeth, getting the coffee ready, etc.

- Write out all of the steps in painstaking detail—for example, if you're writing the steps for getting the coffee ready, you may write: open the cupboard on the left, remove coffee from shelf. Measure out four cups of ground beans (my wife likes coffee), take out coffee filter... you see where I am going here.

- Do the same with whatever activity you chose.

- Repeat this exercise again with another mundane activity—go into deep detail. Then repeat again with one more mundane activity.

- Read all of the steps over and become mind-boggled—can you believe how many steps it takes to complete a task that you don't even think about anymore?!

- Revel in the pure staggering abilities of your nervous system to combine all these steps into a habit—the steps you've just listed out are part of habits you already have. Amazing, right?

- Think about how you can leverage this same power to create even better habits that will lead you toward growth—now that you see you already have many engrained habits, it's time to consider whether these habits are serving you or not. If they're not, it's time to create some new, more empowering habits.

- Make a list of empowering habits you'd like to create—for example, drinking a glass of water when you first wake up, going to bed earlier, setting your alarm across the room so you have to get up to turn it off, etc.

- Choose one of the new empowering habits you want to create and write out each step you'll need to take from start to finish—do this just like you did with the mundane activities above. Then start taking action on this new habit (and one year from now, you can look back and see how all these steps have dissolved into an easy, thoughtlessly awesome activity that helps propel you toward growth in your life).

LITTLE VICTORIES

"The key to realizing a dream is to focus not on success... but significance! Then...even small steps and little victories along your path will take on greater meaning."

—MARKESA YEAGER

"Know thy self, know thy enemy. A thousand battles, a thousand victories."

—SUN TZU

When living (or on the path toward living) an inspired life, it's easy to get caught up in your biggest goals. You can look at a "finish line" as the ultimate goal: losing x pounds, being fully confident, writing the book, getting the perfect job, finding the right person, leaving a legacy, becoming the President of the company, being anointed Warrior King of all the Fraggles, etc. No problem there, but most of the time the end-goal is looked at as the ONLY goal.

Therein lies the rub. All along this path toward transformation there are a multitude of steps you'll need to take. Follow with me on this metaphor, if you will:

You're going to climb Mt. Everest—that is your big goal. Seems like a good idea, and you've got nothing going on this Saturday anyway, besides laundry. But you can't just think of "climbing Mt. Everest" as the only goal, because it's not.

So let's think about all the other things you'll need to do to accomplish that goal: start hiking smaller mountains first, or at least start some sort of conditioning routine (definitely need to get moving, watching Survivor Man marathons on TV won't cut it). Eat a proper diet. Dive into a stretching routine. Figure out how you're going to book a flight to Nepal and take off the time from work. Make sure your house and pet cicadas are taken care of while you're away. Grow an awesome beard and mustache (got to look the part). Purchase some extremely warm layers of clothing. Probably get some hiking poles and better shoes (Air Yeezys and flip-flops won't work). Hire a Sherpa, and so on.

And if you didn't notice, those are only some of the steps you'll need to take before you can even set foot on the mountain!

Then you would need to fly there, book a guide to get you to base camp (I doubt your GPS will work on the mountain), and then you'll need to spend time getting acclimated to the altitude, and then...I think you're getting the gist.

In any worthwhile dream or big vision, there are a gazillion-jillion (I might've stolen that phrase from my son, Isaac) precursor things you need to accomplish before you can "get there." If all you do is keep your eyes on the peak, and don't take the time to notice the little victories along the way, you will get frustrated, disenchanted, burned out, and most likely give up before you get that far.

The flip side to that is if you look at this huge list of little things you must do to prepare for the big goal, you could get intimidated and never even start. This makes it all the more important to acknowledge when you've moved forward along your path. You should become cognizant of all the new synapses being created on the road to the big goal. Don't focus solely on the end. (You don't attend a symphony just to hear the final note, right?)

If your big vision is to live your purpose, to follow your calling and to live an inspired life, you can't decide you will *only* pat yourself on the back once you get to the end. There is no "end" on the journey of life (at least not while you're still alive). There will never be a day that you'll think, "Wow, I'm exactly who I want to be, and I probably don't need to do anything else, I'm good. I'm gonna stop now. Let's get back to watching those Fraggles." When you are working toward being your best possible self, that image will evolve as you learn and grow and as your impact expands. If you only looked at the non-existent finish line, why would you want to continue on the journey? Take care of your dreams by acknowledging that it will take an infinite amount of smaller wins to keep you moving.

In her book, *The Progress Principle*, Author, Teresa Amabile discusses the extensive research she conducted on this topic. They sampled more than two-hundred-thirty people working on creative endeavors, and had them fill out a survey at the end of each work day. They crunched the data to find out which factors helped create what the participants called a "good day." In the end, they had more than twelve-thousand surveys (amounting to twelve-thousand days of work). They found that one main factor in the creation of a "good day" stood out among the rest. When participants denoted progress toward meaningful work on any given day, that had the biggest correlation to a day that was viewed as a positive one.[1]

Another example comes from the police force in Richmond, British Columbia, Canada. The innovative police force there had a large goal to decrease youth crime, so they sent their officers out on the streets with this goal. However, they armed them with "positive tickets" to issue when they noticed a youth in the district acting within the confines of the law and making good choices. The tickets were actually coupons for free hamburgers, movie admission or hockey tickets at local venues. They took this progress principle and started celebrating small victories. If a teen was spotted crossing the road during the walk sign and not running across during an in-opportune moment, they received one of these positive tickets. If someone was spotted picking up litter, they got a tick-

1. Amabile, Teresa and Kramer, Steven. *The Progress Priciple.* Boston, MA: Harvard Business Review Press, 2011. Print

et. If they were driving great, they could get pulled over and given a positive ticket. These little celebrations equated to big victories in the long run. Repeat crime offender instances dropped by 95% and there was a drastic decrease in street racing and, therefore, street racing deaths (The police had come to expect about four deaths per year due to street racing before this initiative and there hasn't been a single such occurrence in the past eight years). The police leveraged positive reinforcement by celebrating little victories along the way, which allowed for a much larger final result. (Read more about this movement at postivetickets.com.)

How can you implement this in your life? Let's say, for example, you want to write a novel. You should celebrate when you finish, absolutely. But you should also celebrate when you start. And when you sit down at the computer to write or jot some lines in your notebook. And when you edit the last paragraph (or delete a chapter because it was just really, really lame). And when you take the time to sit and think about what to write. I'm not implying that you should pop champagne every time you pick up a pen (wouldn't get too much done that way, unless your big dream is to drink a lot of champagne), but a simple pat-on-the-back, a self-acknowledgement, a bit of encouragement, or a dose of congratulations are definitely in order.

When you celebrate the little victories, you are plowing a route to more and more little victories, and your brain and nervous system will hunger for more causes to celebrate. You will literally change your physiology. When you acknowledge accomplishments, your body secretes serotonin, oxytocin, endorphins and dopamine (chemicals related to happiness and well-being). You are also building more receptors for these chemicals. At the same time, you create more neural synapses (more on that in a later chapter), making it easier to "do" whatever it is you are "doing." When you celebrate successes, you are creating a positive feedback loop, making it easier to have more and more successes and to feel better and better about them! You will automatically create more and more opportunities to secrete those feel-good chemicals. This feedback loop can go on and on and on.

Let's dive into these chemicals a bit more...

Dopamine is a motivator. When you are experiencing something tremendously positive or euphoric (best steak ever, best run ever, accomplished a victory, won an award, etc.) dopamine is surging. Dopamine is a huge player in the internal reward system you have in place. When you do something good, you are rewarded with dopamine. A lack of dopamine has also been connected to Alzheimer's disease and Schizophrenia (pretty cool that you can help decrease the chance for these conditions by giving yourself a pat on the back a bit more often). Another great fact, the harder you "work" toward a goal, the more difficult it seems to accomplish the goal, and the higher the surges of dopamine along your path as you achieve the little victories. Setting big goals and working toward them allows for a higher dose of dopamine.

Serotonin is at its peak when you feel successful. This chemical flows when you have a feeling of significance. When you accomplish something, you get a jolt of serotonin to help you feel important. Practicing gratitude also helps serotonin flow. This applies to being grateful for things you have, places you've been and things you've accomplished. Serotonin also helps regulate sleep, memory, learning, and assists in intestinal regulation (pretty cool that you can aid your digestive system and sleep better by congratulating yourself from time-to-time).

Oxytocin is "the connection" chemical. It helps create intimacy and trust in relationships. Oxytocin helps you feel bonded to others and to your world. Oxytocin is released when you receive a gift. Oxytocin is released when you do something nice for someone else, or when you feel love toward another, or have empathy, or when you shake hands or give a hug to a friend, or when you are just being a "good person." Additionally, oxytocin helps decrease inflammation and assists in wound healing (pretty cool that when you allow yourself to spread some love you can decrease inflammation in your body and help yourself heal faster).

Endorphins help you recover from stress and make you feel good. Endorphins are your body's way to fight your perception of pain. Your body will release endorphins to try to help get you through stressful situations, but you can give it a kick-start simply by smiling or laughing. When you take a step back after a victory and smile or laugh, you release endorphins to help you feel even better (pretty cool that when you look back on what you've done, endorphins are released and you experience a bit of a "runner's high").

These chemicals—dopamine, serotonin, oxytocin, endorphins—help you move forward on your path to living an inspired life. In fact they can be the key to transforming your life. And you can tap into them anytime by acknowledging the steps along the journey a bit more often. So take the time to pat yourself on the back and smile at your victories (you will find there are going to be plenty when you look for them). Because, let's be honest, it's a pretty damn big deal to get a rock-solid Sherpa hired (maybe leave a Yelp review to make it easier for the next Sherpa-searcher).

PURPOSELY POSITIVE EXERCISE: CHECKLIST OF CELEBRATION

Grab your notebook and do the following:

1. This weekend (or next, I promise I won't follow you around to see if you're adhering to my instructions) think of what you need/want to accomplish, then write out all the steps it will take to get the "job done"—include even the little steps.

2. Draw little boxes next to each step

3. When you complete a step, draw a big checkmark or happy face in the box next to it—do this for each step until all of them are complete.

4. Give yourself a tiny gift for each checkmark/smile you earn—for example, a bit of chocolate, a latte, pat on the back, a shot of Jameson Irish Whiskey... (Just kidding on that last one; you probably have stuff to do today still). The

point is to celebrate the small victories as you move from point A to point Z.

BIG IMPACT?

"Dripping water hollows out stone not through force but through persistence."

—Ovid

I remember once sitting in a seminar and an awesome speaker (Dr. Devin Vrana) stated that in order to win perceived battles, you could decide to put on your (as she called them) "Hulk Smash gloves" and get angry, and try to inflict a change by force (verbal or otherwise), and to let your passion boil over into conflict...or you could go another route. I love that analogy, possibly because I have two boys and one of them is a stickler for all things Superhero. I remember thinking of buying him these giant green gloves that would spout out, "HULK SMASH" anytime you hit them together, or against a board, or against another human (which is why I thought actually purchasing them would not be good for his brother, mother, myself, or anyone else he could imagine as a 'bad guy,' and he has a great imagination).

You could put on your "smash gloves" and start hitting, flailing, trying to IMPACT the things/people that you feel have wronged you, and in doing so, damage them and yourself. No matter the cushion in those gloves, if you hit something with enough force it's going to hurt. Once (aka "multiple times") in high school while playing soccer, I got beat by the guy I was covering who then went on to score. Angry, I popped up in front of the goalpost and de-

63

cided the best way to help my team at that moment was to punch the goalpost. The post didn't break in half like I thought it would (imagine that), but my hand sure swelled up (I still have a rather large middle knuckle on my right hand thanks to this decision). I made an impact for sure, but not really the one I was going for.

You don't usually "win" when you decide to smash. That type of impact won't create lasting, positive change. The impact will be felt, but it won't bring forth your desire to lighten the world.

When you decide to make an impact on your own life—get healthy, join a gym, create a new habit of reading every night, give up pizza, be a better person—many times you try to start by making a BIG impact. Sometimes that actually works: some people can make big decisions and then stick to it forever and life is awesome (well hooray for whoever "they" are, but I haven't met a "they" yet).

For most people, deciding to make a BIG impact may succeed in the short term, until the rocket explodes and they shatter back down to Earth. The same is true if you want to follow your inspiration to make the world a better place. Save the whales, the zebras, the duck-billed platypuses, or maybe just change your mentality.

You can't sustain the force of a large impact.

The initial results are usually great: you feel better. You're on the right path. You're striving, but then...you burn out. You hurt. You give up. You give in. This isn't just evident in the physical health realm, either. The same thing applies on aims to make an impact on the world at large.

For example, you decide you want to be more positive, so you wake up the next few days extremely chipper and with huge grins all around. Then you hit turbulence, and stress happens (stress is a part of life, if you don't have any stress, I hate to break it to you, but you are in fact...dead). If you step into making changes with over-exuberance and devil-may-care attitudes, it can be a great start, but will become unsustainable. You will hit the proverbial wall. Trying to inspire big changes in your life or the world at large will be unsuccessful if you're attempting for the meteoric impact right away. "But, what about so-and-so who invented the Wunder-Wiggity-Widget and overnight became a huge success?" your mind asks.

Well, Smarty-Pants, the overnight success, who made-a-huge-impact NEVER truly happened overnight. What you assume is he made this impact in the blink of an eye. But what really happened is he toiled, practiced, read, clawed, fell, got up, fell again, over and over, only to finally hit the goal. To the rest of us, his success was "waved into fruition" out of nowhere at all with a magical wand (except that wand doesn't really exist). He worked on their big impact over and over and over again until his success "happened."

"It takes 20 years to become an overnight success."

—EDDIE CANTOR

Behind the scenes, successful people have been working on creating this impact for quite some time, yet you only see the crater left by their awesomeness (and not the creation of the meteor). The same goes for the guy who lost a hundred pounds and became the next big CrossFit Phenom or American Ninja Warrior; he toiled and worked and strove with a ton of effort to finally make this seemingly huge impact. There is a plethora of proof in the "Struggle-rific" chapter of this book, but here are a couple examples to whet your appetite:

It took Bill Gates nearly two decades to become an "overnight" dot-com billionaire. Apple was established in 1976, didn't really get on the map until 1984, and didn't really become the giant it is today until the iMac, iPod and iPhone were invented.

The Beatles played in dive bars and small venues for years before they were recognized by the media. Mick Jagger called dozens and dozens of radio DJs *begging* to get his demo played.

You wake up one day and decide you want to change the world. You know you will. You have the calling. That decision is a big impact, but to put such a noble goal into play, it's going to take an enormous amount of smaller impacts and ripples and impacts and ripples and... which is why I'm suggesting that in order to follow your inspiration (or to get inspired in the first place), you must strive to first make a heckuva lot of little impacts.

Start with a decision. That ripples into ideas for actions. Where to start? Reading this is already making an impact, and in the extreme sense, it could impact you in different ways. It could profoundly change your outlook. Or, you may think the book was rubbish and decide you could do it better. The world will be impacted either way, by your absorption of the genius in this book (tongue planted firmly in cheek), or by sharing your genius in your own way with the world, in whatever form you choose.

In following your inspiration, the goal is to leave your mark on the universe, to leave it better than you found it. That may sound awesome, but it's also crazy-scary-daunting. So just start by taking the first step. Let your soul flow. Let your inspiration light and guide you in the direction you are heading. Don't stare at the "finish line," just follow your feet. Each step you take in allowing your spirit to guide you is one of those small impacts and ripples, and each of those add up to huge change, drastic impact, and world improvement.

Right now it's about opening that door and letting that inspiration out, or if need be, opening the top and letting some light in. For example, if your goal is to invent the world's first flying bicycle that also pours an amazing cup of coffee and shaves your face on the way to work (O.K., that might not be your goal, but feel free to use the idea, it isn't patented...yet). Your first step will be drawing the dang thing on paper. Draw it. Imagine it. Visualize it. Decide why you need it. Or maybe just sit quietly and ask yourself, "what is my soul trying so desperately to tell me?" Look deep down, find your passion, uncover your purpose and see just how bright that star shines (no matter how long it has been tied down or how strong those chains are).

Start your gigantic impact by taking that first step, whatever it is for you. And as you will read throughout this book, it's not acceptable to wait until you have "the perfect shoes" (or gloves, for that matter) to take that step. Continually achieving little victories will combine to create your big impact.

PURPOSELY POSITIVE EXERCISE:
SMALL THING, BIG IMPACT

The purpose of this exercise is to help you see how big impacts can come from small places. Grab your notebook and do the following:

- Think back to someone in your past who had a large impact on your life.

- At the time, whatever she did seemed quite small, but bring to mind how much of an impact she had on your present and future.

- Was it an elementary school teacher who had a small comment that propelled your confidence?

- A coach who taught you something little that stuck with you for your entire life?

- An childhood friend you may have lost touch with but taught you a profound thing with a small gesture?

- More than likely it was not a singular event, so call to mind at least a few.

- Write a thank you note or email to that person, you don't even have to send it.

- Acknowlege how they made such a large impact on your life in such a seemingly small instance.

WORRY WORTH WARTS?

"Worry does not empty tomorrow of its sorrow, it empties today of its strength."

—CORRIE TEN BOOM

Humans have a tremendous ability to figure things out. We create tiny pieces of plastic and metal that can hold an unfathomable amount of information. We needed a way to stop all of our family members from dying at very young ages, so we invented a way to clean and sanitize our drinking water. We needed a way to see the world and discover new places, so we invented the airplane and the train and the automobile. In fact, we get so bored with our lives at times, we buy puzzles that take hours/days/weeks to solve, just to keep our minds busy. We are amazingly adept at fixing and solving things (we've even invented imaginary numbers to solve equations that couldn't be solved without them...thanks, Algebra). We are so good at solving problems, we've decided as a group to create new problems for ourselves, and we allow our amazing brains to churn and turn on these imaginary problems all day (or at least for long periods of time). We stew and brew over what-ifs, how-comes, and "it'd be-so-horrible-if *blankety-blank* occurs."

We love our imaginary worry friends. I know you don't really think your worries are your friends, but if they aren't...why do you spend so much time with them? You ruminate over things that haven't happened, that may happen, and things that more than likely *won't* happen. You run through scenarios over and over in your mind, soul and heart, and these scenarios are based on...nothing concrete.

At least your imaginary friends as children would have tea parties with you. Worry-friends just drain your energy and steal your resolve. They are thieves. They rob you of positivity, motivation and inspiration, and you can only blame yourself for inviting them over in the first place. Sure, they may have shown up out of the blue, like a creepy door-to-door vacuum salesman, but instead of saying, "No thank you," you invited those annoying worries in, feeding them dinner and asking them to spend the next few weeks at your house for free.

When you "anti-dream" (worrying is basically the exact opposite of dreaming), you lock your true self up, and you pluck away at the feathers on the wings of hope. Truth: bad things are going to happen. Pretty profound huh? Bad things happen and that is a fact. Another truth: good things happen too, and if you take the time to open your eyes you'll see that the good VASTLY outnumbers the bad. However, you can still decide to sit around, pull your hair out with anxiety, chew your fingernails until they're nubbins, or grind your teeth until even eating Jello is hard to accomplish. You could do all of these behaviors and swim in a gigantic pool of worry-tears, and it would accomplish ABSOLUTELY NOTHING.

If you are just going to take time to hang out with your imaginary worry-friend, why make him a hideous monster? Do you know what this monster gives you in return? Worrying causes a plethora of pleasant experiences, such as: dry mouth, dizziness, difficulty swallowing, headaches, a faster heartbeat, muscle aches, nausea, shortness of breath, trembling, suppression of the immune system, digestive disorders, and reproductive disorders (sounds like the side effects of a new wonder drug, doesn't it?), just to name a few

Worry causes stress, and when your brain is stressed, the prefrontal cortex (the most advanced portion of your brain, responsible for regulation of thought, emotion and putting together positive, goal-oriented behaviors) gets "turned down," and the amygdala (a much more primitive portion of your brain, responsible for recognizing a threat and sounding the alarm) gets "turned up." Ordinarily an impulse will hit the amygdala and a "reaction" will be initiated, but it will go up to the prefrontal cortex for further review first. More often than not, your prefrontal cortex will take in the information and extrapolate what to do next, usually putting the kibosh on the amygdala's antics. But when the prefrontal cortex is turned down, you react the way you would expect a primitive mind to...hastily. In this way, even "small" stresses over time can cause reactions (hormonal secretions, blood sugar elevation, etc.) that would be more suited to a serious danger, rather than a small worry.

Prolonged periods of this type of internal environment will zap years off your life (if you've seen *The Princess Bride*, you probably pictured that machine in the Pit of Despair, and if you haven't seen the movie...shame on you). Sounds like great fun, right? Of course not! But you return again and again to this torture because, in some ways, your brain is addicted to the worry.

Studies have shown that worrying secretes cortisol. Cortisol is the stress hormone, which—when left unchecked—causes a multitude of negative health effects. Cortisol also causes dopamine production. We went over dopamine in a previous chapter, and it's definitely beneficial, but dopamine is more of a "me" chemical. Dopamine reinforces thinking about yourself, and it also has a tendency to lean you away from social situations and more toward yourself.

Your worries could be resolved easier if you had a trusted friend or family member go over your unfounded fears, but when you produce too much cortisol, and therefore too much dopamine, you tend to avoid those situations and ruminate in solitude.

Excess cortisol leads to excess dopamine, which helps ensure the worrier is truly alone with their worries.

Additionally, when you have a cortisol spike, the intention is to heighten your fight-or-flight senses, in order to avoid danger or accomplish you task. When you replay the worry tape over and over, there isn't a resolution. There isn't an accomplishment and there isn't a finish line. So the short-term benefitting chemicals run rampant and DESTROY you long term.

Have the courage to say "no more." You need to overcome your imaginary worry-friends.

Worries will crop up from time-to-time, but you must use it as intended: to spark a decision, forecast your growth and see the light at the end of the tunnel. You can train yourself to get your prefrontal cortex to stop checking out and instead help you make decisions to overcome worry and find solutions for the root cause.

Your journey is too important to give worry another second of your valuable time.

PURPOSELY POSITIVE EXERCISE: LIST OF LAMENTS

Grab your notebook and do the following:

- Think about something you're worrying about—write it down.

- Now go as far as you can down the road of what the absolute worst case scenario could be—really use your imagination and have some fun here. Exaggerate to your pen's content. For example,

- What if you don't get the job?

- Your family will probably call you names, throw tomatoes at your car, and go on your local news in order to divulge your deepest, most embarrassing secrets.

- The local town will all tune in because your failure is so riveting.

- It will become national news, you'll be forced to move to a tiny island in the middle of the Pacific Ocean where you'll realize you have a horrible allergy to sand and sun and you will waste away for the rest of time...

- Go there with it (but you have to write your own worst case scenario, you can't steal that one).

- Why? Because the more ground you cover in the worry train, the more you realize that the small what ifs are just as plausible as the gigantic crazy ones. Yet neither has happened.

- Hopefully, you'll realize that you get to decide what to think about your future, and the worrying is not going to get you to your ideal destination.

- Now write out all the positive things that could happen on the other end of the spectrum—use your imagination and have fun with this one too. From now on, when you start to worry, instead of allowing yourself to hop on the "worst-case-scenario" train, stop yourself and write out/focus on the positive things that could happen if you got on the "best-case-scenario" train.

HUMILITY ≠ HUMILIATION

"Talent is God given. Be humble. Fame is man-given. Be grateful. Conceit is self-given. Be Careful."

—JOHN WOODEN

"Honesty is grounded in humility and indeed in humiliation, and in admitting exactly where we are powerless."

—DAVID WHYTE

Did you know that public speaking ranks highest among all fears in America? Of course you did. Everyone knows that. For a huge percentage of the population, the fear of public speaking is paralyzing. It's my contention this fear is rooted in humiliation. We are all afraid of being humiliated. Fear of embarrassment limits you in so many areas of your life. Sometimes your fear of what others may think stops you from doing amazing things. Yet humiliation is a very real and crippling emotion. So, like most humans, you avoid humiliation at all costs.

Although the words sound similar, humility is much different than humiliation. Humility is defined as a modest view of one's own importance. It's about not letting Ego or Id run the ship entirely. On that note, let's get into a little Freudian psychology (don't worry, I won't get into the Mother complex/Father complex deal).

According to Sigmund Freud, personalities have three different elements: the Id, the Superego, and the Ego.

The Id is concerned with pleasure. The Id is primitive and impulsive. It's the infantile portion of your mind. The Id is the little voice in your head saying, "go ahead and eat the whole box of donuts," or "you should totally run outside in your birthday suit simply to feel the wind against your skin!" My son did this once when he was three...during a housewarming party we were having at our house, true story. We were in our kitchen discussing the problem we were having potty-training our dogs when a friend said, "Don't worry about your dog, your son is running naked and peeing in the back yard." My son's reasoning? "I just like the way the wind feels on my skin!" The Id is concerned at all times with seeking pleasure, and not with repercussions. Clearly my son was letting his Id run free.

The Ego works to balance the Id with the external world. It is still concerned with personal pleasure and avoids pain, but works to devise realistic strategies to obtain that pleasure. The Ego looks at options and considers the best choice to fulfill desires. The Ego balances the Id with these ideas.

For example, while running outside to "feel the air" would be nice, maybe you could at least wear some shorts. Another example: "If I eat one donut now, I could grab a few more and bring them back to my desk to eat later." The Ego's drive is still self-gratification, but in a less impulsive way.

The Superego balances the Id and Ego with morality and judgements of right and wrong. The Superego is kind of like the angel on your shoulder whispering in your ear: "Don't eat the entire box of donuts, save some for other people." Or, "It would be nice to feel the air, but now is not the time to go running outside, you're in the middle of dinner with your family and the new neighbor (who happens to be a pastor) and it might not be so appreciated." The Superego is always looking at the "right" thing to do in all situations.

To be clear, you need to use all three parts of your personality in order to live a successful, happy life. You cannot function on one alone. The key is to balance them all together, to use them in unison to help see you through situations, to help you think with your heart and your head. And when they get out of balance, doom is on the horizon.

What does any of this have to do with the title of this chapter? Great question! Here's the answer: Strive for humility, lest you end up humiliated. If you let your Ego or Id rule the roost, you put your desires above all others. You may obtain some success along your quest; you may accumulate honors, trophies, ribbons or whatever else they are handing out these days, but eventually you'll realize you think of yourself too much, and then you'll lead a lonely life. If the Id runs the ship, even more so you can cultivate some enjoyment, but eventually (it probably wouldn't take too long), you would end up humiliating yourself. If you lean into Ego too much, the result will still be humiliation, it will just take a while longer than if you let Id take the reins. Or, if you weren't humiliated, but let Ego drive for too long, you would become self-centered and risk separating yourself from society by your own volition. Put yourself first all the time and the inevitable outcome will be getting "knocked down a peg or two" on the ladders of life you're attempting to climb.

The Superego is where humility comes into play. The Superego can keep you on the correct side of the morality line. If you lean too much into the Superego however, you'll move beyond humble and can fall into self-depreciation. There is such a thing as being TOO altruistic. What good is it to others if you continually hurt yourself in the process? That just isn't a viable life.

As C.S. Lewis put so succinctly, *"Humility is not thinking less of ourselves, it is thinking about ourselves less."* Being humble is vastly different than being self-destructive. You definitely need to think of your own wants and needs in order to survive, and what good can you do for others if you are not surviving? (Right?)

I also believe that a large portion of the population hold themselves back for fear that showing who they truly are might cause others to feel less about *themselves*. They don't hold themselves back for fear of humiliation; they hold themselves back under the guise of humility. They play small in order to fit in, to not rock the boat, to ensure they get approval from others. They believe that in order to be HUMBLE, they need to keep their true creativity, their true genius, true passions, true skills and true selves locked up. They go through life at 70% of their abilities, knowing they can do pretty well, but are afraid of going 100% because "what would people think?" and "Isn't that boastful?" and "You can't do your best if you want to be humble"... right?

Wrong! Minimizing yourself in order to gain influence is not humility, it is, in actuality, self-serving. Hiding who you truly are doesn't help others, and most certainly doesn't allow you to improve the world around you. It's your choice to hide or shine your gifts. However, I do believe that when those gifts were given to you, they weren't meant to be hidden. You need to give thanks for them and share your soul with the world.

True humility is leading with your gifts, in all their glory, and being grateful that they were bestowed upon you. True humility is working to improve yourself in order to contribute to those around you (and that can't be done at 70% of your true ability). It isn't about being boastful or exaggerating who you truly are, but rather living as who you are meant to be, for the greater good.

In life, balance and moderation are key. Work with all three of Freud's personality aspects to better serve your family, yourself and your world. I believe if you lead with humility, while also considering your own needs (and having some fun in the process), you will be living your life completely and on-purpose—the way you were meant to live all along. Good ol' Siggy (don't worry, Freud would be cool with me calling him that) provided a lot of insight into what propels you, but you get to choose how to do the actual driving.

PURPOSELY POSITIVE EXERCISE:
FREUD'S FRIENDLY FACES

Grab your notebook and do the following:

- Draw an image of what you think your Ego, Id and SuperEgo look like—have fun with this!

- Underneath each image, write some instances where each would be useful—for example, your Ego may be useful when deciding whether to eat the box of cookies yourself, or share them with someone else.

- Answer the following questions about the images you just drew:

  ○ When do you think you should lead with your Ego?

  ○ How about your Id or SuperEgo?

  ○ Which would get more done, and impact humanity in a positive, profound way for a longer period of time?

  ○ Why?

PERFEKSHUN

"I am careful not to confuse excellence with perfection. Ex-
cellence I can reach for; perfection is God's business."

—Michael J. Fox

The desire for the perfect opportunity has most assuredly de-
stroyed more amazing discoveries than any plague in history.
Just think about all the amazing ideas that people have, the songs
or art they want to create, but they wait until the ideal time to begin or to release their creativity. That "perfect" opportunity may
never come along, and so all these amazing ideas and creations never even make it off the starting blocks.

Ever heard the story of the invention of the Post-it note? In
1968, Spencer Silver, an employee at the 3M Company, was trying
to create a super-strong adhesives to aid in building planes. Instead,
he accidentally created a very weak adhesive. Rather than give up
on the "failed" product, Silver kept sharing it with other employ-
ees. It wasn't until 1973 when the product finally found a use.
Art Fry, a chemical engineer and member of a church choir in
St. Paul, Minnesota, approached Silver about his weak adhesive.
He needed something to keep his song page markers separated in
his hymn book. They realized they could put the "failed adhesive"
on a piece of paper and stick it to anything and it would come off
with ease—and the Post-It Note was created. Even more amazing,
the company didn't think it would be very popular, so they shelved

it until 1977. The product was a flop at first, but they reintroduced it with more gusto and it has since become one of the top five best-selling office supply products ever made. All because of Mr. Silver's imperfect accident.[1]

In my life, I have struggled with perfectionism. It took me quite a while (years, in fact) to sit down and write this book. Thoughts in my head swirled around about needing it to be the perfect time, or having to wait until I had some monumentally impactful success that the world as a whole knew about. I needed the perfect theme, the perfect audience, the perfect voice. I held myself back under the guise of perfection. The funny thing was, I have been writing my entire life. I had a four-hundred-page journal (it wasn't a diary, thank you very much) in high school. I took creative writing classes whenever I could. My first major in college was Journalism (until I found I couldn't be as creative in that writing-style as I truly wanted to be). I've always had some sort of notebook nearby to jot things down in. I just didn't share my writing with too many people, unless the "perfect" phrase or sentence popped into my head. I was afraid. Perfectionism was my mask.

Obviously, I've gotten over that somewhat, or you wouldn't be reading this now. The more I learned about self-improvement and success, the more I realized that no one could ever be perfect. This book isn't perfect by any stretch. But I realized that if I truly wanted to share myself with the world, if I wanted to help others, then one of the best ways was to be vulnerable and not hide my imperfections. I realized that the mask of perfectionism I was hiding behind was actually just smothering my gifts. The lofty mantle of perfectionism that I held onto needed to crumble.

Perfectionism has been looked at as a positive trait over the past few generations. I'm sure, in some ways, you admire the people that you've given the label "Perfectionist" to, and they seem like wonderful individuals. They are motivated, passionate, courageous and meticulous. Perfectionists are meticulous. They are successful and they are meant to be idols, or so you'd think. The problem is, "per-

---

1. *http://www.todayifoundout.com/index.php/2011/11/post-it-notes-were-invented-by-accident/*

fectionism" is not the same as having a "strong work ethic." There is a HUGE difference between the two.

A strong work ethic is truly admirable. It's marvelous to strive for excellence or mastery, and that cannot be accomplished without a strong work ethic. A strong work ethic enables people to get things done, to improve their craft, and to help others in the process. Perfection, on the other hand, screams of selfishness. Perfection is never good enough. Nothing in the world is truly perfect. And honestly, the entire world is based upon your perception of it. Something that you deem as "perfect" is probably garbage to someone else. (If you need proof, remember someone thought *Gangnam Style* was the perfect song when it was released).

Perfectionism is an absolute lie. Many times you'll wait until you think things are "perfect" before you take a chance. You hide behind the veil of perfection and ostensibly sit in a corner and suck your thumb because you are too afraid to take that first step. You may chastise yourself for not being perfect, which then allows you to stay down, to bury your light, hide your gifts and, ultimately, stay exactly where you are. Perfectionism is actually rooted in shame and fear. You hold onto an idea or creation until it is "perfect," when in actuality, the motive for doing so is you're afraid others might see its flaws, and will, therefore think you're flawed.

After all, it's so much easier to hide behind trying to be perfect than to actually just TRY. To truly "strive for perfection" just opens the door to lying down, taking a long nap, and just giving up all together. If you truly know, as I am sure you do, that perfection is impossible, how hard is it to "give it your all" if you know it won't be perfect? Many times you opt to never start in the first place. That is exactly what I was doing by convincing myself I had to be perfect to write this book, so I never sat down to even begin typing it, until I took off the perfection mask.

I completely believe that having HUGE goals is necessary in order for inspiration to flourish, for you to succeed and make an impact on the world. Strive for excellence and keep stretching how excellent you can be. But aiming for perfection is nothing but an artificial pursuit. In all your endeavors, do the best you possibly can, and you will notice that your "best" grows and grows and grows. Excellence, success, positivity—all of these things can expand and improve.

The true meaning of perfection calls to mind a cold, immovable, solid...end. And truly, if you're following your passions, you don't want them to end. You don't want a truly finished product. You want creativity and happiness and purpose to allow for continual refinement. One of the most amazing things about being human is the ability to re-imagine, amend, build on, and enhance things constantly. You will never be "out of stock" in your ability to build amazing things, share new thoughts or create beautiful art.

But what if, theoretically, someone actually created THE PERFECT cup of coffee, or THE PERFECT book, or THE PERFECT anything? You can't improve upon perfect. It's done. If, for example, you ever connected to yourself so wholeheartedly that next Tuesday, you uncovered your purpose and you found a way to deliver it perfectly... what would you do the following Tuesday? (I say 'the following Tuesday' because I'm assuming you'll have some amazing parties for the six days following your discovery and perfect delivery). The next logical step would be to give up. Once perfection is attained, wouldn't everything become boring? And that is not what you're here for.

"Striving for perfection" is an exercise in futility. Your purpose is not futile. Don't hold yourself back by trying to be perfect. Don't be so delusional as to think whatever you create will be perfect. Hopefully you are in-tune with your passion, and you combine that with inspiration and produce excellence. I have no doubt that's what you'll do, but the beauty of excellence is you can continue to improve and excel. So go for growth. Strive for beauty. Aim for inspiration, and as Michael J. Fox said, keep perfection in the hands of God.

PURPOSELY POSITIVE EXERCISE:
DEFINE YOUR PERFECT DAY

Grab your notebook and do the following:

- Write out your perfect day, from the moment you wake up to the moment you go to bed—be vivid.

- Explain all of the details.

- Consider: how does that day look? Sound? Feel?

- Now think back to when you were 10 years old, and, again, define your perfect day (at that age).

- Write it out in all its glory.

- Now think of yourself at age 98 and, again, write out your perfect day.

- What does your perfect day look like then?

- Compare and contrast these visualizations—where are things different? Where are they the same?

- I bet there will be some major differences. I'm also sure there will be some solid similarities. Especially in the "how does that day feel" department.

- Make a list of all of the feelings you wrote down in all three of your ideal day scenarios—the feelings you have connected to these images is what you should be striving for. This is your starting point every day.

- Combine striving for excellence with the wonderful feelings you experienced and you will truly be unstoppable.

X-TURNAL VALIDATION
&
A W(HOLE) LOTTA LOVE

"What the superior man seeks is in himself; what the small man seeks is in others."

—CONFUCIUS

I f perfectionism is a lie you tell yourself that inevitably holds you back, then external validation is the concrete you put in your pockets to keep you there. The desire for validation from the external world is incredibly common. As Jess Walter put it, *"The whole world is sick...We've all got this pathetic need to be seen. We're a bunch of toddlers trying to get attention."* There is no harm in wanting to be acknowledged for your successes, or just to know that others actually "see" you. But when you attempt to derive your value based on how someone else appraises you, it will inhibit your true genius.

The concept of external validation is flawed. How can you look to people outside yourself to prove that you are worthy on the inside? It's basically akin to the following math problem: "If Sally plants 6 apple trees, and David likes to drive his Smart Car on his neighbor's lawn, how many tacos would the average sperm whale ingest on a cloudy Friday in September?" When you look outside yourself to fix, validate or solve something on the inside, there is no solution.

Where does this need come from? You probably have never had someone look at you and say, *"Hey, just so you know, you aren't good enough. You're lacking in so many areas it's redonkulous."* I also refuse to believe that you were created with a giant crater —or hole of emptiness—inside in order to fill yourself up with the adoration of others. Yet, maybe you feel that you're lacking in some way. You feel unworthy; you have a lower self-esteem than you should. You've decided (slowly, over time, or just this morning after eating your Pop-Tarts) that you're not good enough to have an amazing life. That's an important distinction. It was a decision, and sometimes that same decision is made as part of your daily routine. You may not like thinking it was a decision, because that puts responsibility on you. You may feel your low self-worth was forced on you by the outside world. People may have treated you like dirt in your past. You may have been bullied or had your feelings trod upon. So there may be some nuggets of truth in outside factors helping to create low self-worth, but also realize that it's your decision at each moment whether you continue telling yourself that sad story or create a new one for a much happier future. The good news: if you accept it as a decision, you can also realize that decisions are NEVER final.

When I was a wee young lad, my grandma made me eat this horrific cauliflower dish. I DECIDED right then and there I was never going to eat cauliflower as an adult, because it was Satan's shrubbery and is not fit for human consumption. And that decision was FIRM! Until the other day when I saw a video on making "cauliflower fried rice"—with no actual rice—using a bunch of other vegetables to make a main dish. I immediately showed Sheri and said, "We can totally make this!" (Note: we did make it and it was ahh-mazing!) So that firm decision I made years before was trumped by another decision.

You can always make another decision.

The desire for external validation is a need to fill a void, and nothing outside yourself could ever fix anything on the inside. It's like trying to fill your hands with water. No matter how much water is poured into your hands, and no matter how hard you try to hold onto it, eventually the liquid will seep through, and you'll be left empty again, yearning for more. You need something much more solid to hold on to.

So I beg you, don't fall into the trap of thinking that by pursuing your passion, others will finally be happy. You will get recognition. Your self-worth will swell and that "hole" will gain a "w" prefix. You won't suddenly be satiated. Your hunger for validation won't suddenly cease. You will definitely get recognition. Some will undoubtedly be praise, some will be critical, and some will best be described as, "meh." Some won't even notice. But YOUR purpose is not to make others think more highly of you. At least that purpose won't truly inspire any sort of greatness. That validation is not even adequate for a meal. That type of purpose is maybe a single sardine.

I can promise you that if you feel your purpose truly rests with getting others to like you, there will be no substance and you'll certainly leave no legacy.

Confession time: I ~~was~~ am horrible at this. Even as I'm writing this sentence I'm thinking (a little bit) about, "I hope you really like that bit about the Smart Car and the neighbor's lawn." All my life I've somewhat determined my worth based on how others viewed me. At a truly amazing chiropractic conference one December, we each had to get up and talk about our biggest hang up or our biggest advice we could give to the group. I realized I was a complete hypocrite at that moment, because I was going to talk about humility. I was pretty proud of what I thought out, but mainly I chose that topic because I wanted everyone in the room to turn to their neighbor and whisper, *"Wow—he's so humble! It's awesome!"* (maybe with a tear or two in their eye, and maybe throw in a *"and so unbelievably handsome too"* for good measure). Just so I could be thought of as the most humble person in the room. That is most definitely NOT humility. So, yes, I am guilty of this, but I'm working on it, and I have improved by leaps and bounds.

I know firsthand the destruction that can occur when you try to look to the outside for self-worth, and it ain't pretty. When I was about ten-years-old, I got busted for shoplifting some G.I. Joe figures (and this wicked-awesome boat they rode in) from my local Target. They were the newest, and, therefore, coolest, G.I. Joe's available. I couldn't afford them, but I wanted them so my friends would come over to play at my house. I didn't want them badly; I just wanted my friends to see that I had them. Then my amazing action figure prowess would be noticed and I would be validated.

I failed lap swimming in high school (when I had college soccer scouts coming to watch me, but I wasn't allowed to play because I failed *lap swimming*: a class where all you do is swim back and forth in the pool), because I never went to class. I wanted other kids to think I was cool for not going.

I've posted things on Facebook, and then anxiously awaited (and counted) the "likes" so I could feel that I really was "somebody." I'm a thousand percent sure that I wasn't alone in posting my "soul" on social media in the hopes to garner some "likes" and to attach my self-worth to an arbitrary number of social media "friends." It's downright scary the connection between seeking online likes, re-posts and re-tweets and the very real and scathing need for acceptance in real life (or the perceived lack-thereof). The addiction to the virtual "thumbs up" has been shown to have a very deleterious effect on our real lives. Research has shown that cases of depression have been on the rise in a similar rate comparable to the use of social media. The more people use social media for acceptance, the more they're depressed in their real lives.[1]

This isn't just a problem with social media. People use (and even become addicted to) social media for the same reasons I ruined my potential soccer career and shoplifted action figures—we're all striving for external affirmation to fill the crater inside.

Suffice it to say, through some long talks with my wife, my parents, my brother, my counselor, and my own self-discovery, the

---

1. *https://psychcentral.com/blog/does-social-media-cause-depression/*

hole is getting smaller and the need is morphing into a slight want. I'm not saying you shouldn't care what others think. That'd be too cliché, for one, and for two, you should care (some) what others think, especially those you love. And it's definitely O.K. to try to please people, but not if it displeases your own soul, and not if it becomes a driving force in your life. Getting support from people you care about is paramount to your success. They can act as the beams that *help* hold you up, but the foundation needs to come from within yourself.

The desire to please others in order to feel worthy inside can be a brutal hunger, and in getting recognition for it, you're fed...for a short while, only to have the sustenance turn to ash in your mouth and leave you starving and malnourished. Focus on creating healthy soil. Nurture your spirit from the inside. Grow your own self-worth and your acceptance of who you are. It's the only way.

You cannot help the world until you help yourself.

PURPOSELY POSITIVE EXERCISES: SUPER-AWESOME SELF-REALIZATION

Grab your notebook and do the following:

- Take 5 minutes to just stare at yourself in the mirror.

- Write down 50 things that makes you awesome

- No negativity allowed.

- That should barely scratch the surface. Write them all down, and just keep going.

- Answer these questions if you start running out of things:

  ○ What does your mother love about you?

  ○ Your spouse/significant other?

  ○ What are you good at?

  ○ What are you great at?

- ○ What are you getting better at?

- ○ What accomplishments have you had in your lifetime (go way back, think about awards in elementary, middle and high school, even if it was the class clown award)?

- ○ What do you do better than your siblings?

- ○ What sorts of foods are you great at making?

- ○ What would your best friend say about you?

- ○ What would your dog/cat/pet ostrich say about you?

- ○ What is your best feature?

- ○ What are your best traits?

- Come back to this list over the next few weeks and keep on adding things—this list could go on forever, because let's face it... you are pretty damn amazing! Read it whenever you need a reminder.

DREAM. AND THEN...

"All men dream, but not equally. Those who dream by night in the dusty recesses of their minds, wake in the day to find that it was vanity; but the dreamers of the day are dangerous men, for they may act on their dreams with open eyes, to make them possible."

—T.E. LAWRENCE

"The only place success comes before work is in the dictionary."

—VINCE LOMBARDI

If you haven't figured it out yet, this whole "changing yourself, living inspired, making an impact" thing is going to take some work. Dreaming is so important, but the world is full of dreamers who are addicted to the dream but allergic to the work. You must have the courage, the moxie, the spirit, the fortitude, to step toward your dreams. Hoping and praying alone won't cut it.

Dream. It is imperative to make your dreams BIG and amazing. You need to have gigantically bold dreams, and you need to keep having them to push the limits of your imagination. But then you must get to work. There is nothing wrong with a pipe dream... as long as you are ready to lay some pipe.

The good news is that work isn't always blood, sweat and tears. I don't know anyone these days who sing songs in unison with the rest of their crew while they hammer railroad ties into the ground (my image of "work" as a child). But in order to allow your passion to fuel you, first you must fan the flames. You don't decide to become an actor and never read a script. You don't decide to be an N.B.A. player and never practice shooting free throws. You can easily dream of those things. But a dream without work is just vapor: you can't hold it and you can barely even see it.

You need to lay your path brick-by-brick. Those bricks aren't always going to be heavy, although some will be heavier than others. Some days your "brick" might be just taking the time to imagine, to visualize, or to plan your dream. Other days, your brick might be clearing space off of your desk to make room for creativity to blossom. Some bricks may consist of: taking a class at the local community college, reading a new book, hiring a coach, or going to the gym. Other days, these bricks might be standing in front of an audience and getting vulnerable, or delving deep into places you aren't entirely sure are safe for you to go, internally. Each brick is vital, and you're the ONLY one who gets to build the path toward your dreams.

Maybe your path hasn't been too hard so far. Things may have been easy for you up until now. Maybe you're gifted and never needed to study in school. Maybe swinging a golf club just came naturally to you. Well, that's nice. But that is not where the story ends (unless you want to write a really crappy story... "Once upon a time, there was a boy named Timmy who woke up and was amazing at everything. The end"). No one wants to read that story. Even if it has been all roses and gumdrops, or hammocks and ice cold beers (I'll take the latter any day), at some point you're going to have to introduce your nose to the grindstone.

Maybe your life hasn't been so easy. Maybe each day has been a struggle to get by. But I believe God put some amazing things inside each and every one of us, and in order to truly share your gifts with the world (why else would He have put them there in the first place), you need to prod them out and work on them. You need to cultivate, nurture them, and allow them to grow. That isn't going to happen by chance alone. You are a masterpiece, this is true, but you've got to work on molding your clay. Every. Single. Day.

You're NOT a finished product. Ever.

Also, you may be the only person who notices the work you put in (and why would anyone else notice, they should be busy molding their own clay), but that's the point. You work on you because you want to. You don't work toward your dreams and create your art just to have others pay admission to see your statue (a possibility if you truly follow your passion and work with inspiration, for sure... but they don't usually make statues of people while they're still alive). You work toward your dreams because it feels good to do the work and follow where inspiration takes you. Feeling good does not mean easy. In fact, studies show that the most satisfaction is gained through hard work and determination to improve. No one looks back at the "easy" times and feels a tremendous sense of accomplishment for coasting through.

So dream your dream. Lay your bricks one-by-one. Build your statue. Do whatever it takes. But most assuredly, you need to, "get busy livin' or get busy dying"— Andy Dufresne in *The Shawshank Redemption* by Stephen King.

PURPOSELY POSITIVE EXERCISE: DREAM A (CRAZY) LITTLE DREAM

Grab your notebook and do the following:

- What's the craziest (or boldest) dream you've ever had?—not sleeping dream, but dream for yourself and/or your life.

- Write it down, even if it's strange—your pages won't tell on you.

- Why do you think you have this dream?—why did this dream come to you?

- What would happen if that dream just "came true?"—imagine and write down what your life would be like.

LOVIN' OR LABORIN'?

"Trust in what you love, continue to do it, and it will take you where you need to go."

—NATALIE GOLDBERG

"Just don't give up trying to do what you really want to do. Where there is love and inspiration, I don't think you can go wrong."

—ELLA FITZGERALD

I am 199% sure that if I started this chapter with something incredibly lame, like: it's so important to do what you love..." you'd toss this thing right into your Vitamix blender. So I won't start with that.

Even though it is SO important to do what you love in life. (I know its cliché, but don't you think clichés have existed for so long because there's an insurmountable truth in them?) It truly is.

I posted a quote like that on social media, and a friend from high school chimed in with something like, "That's great, but some people still have crappy jobs. Somebody has to be the garbage man." This is true, but the garbage man still chose the job. And in choosing a job, you can choose to not have that job as well. When you make your choice, I can guarantee you'll find things you enjoy about the endeavor.

"If a man is called to be a street sweeper, he should sweep even as Michelangelo painted or Beethoven composed music or Shakespeare wrote poetry. He should sweep streets so well that all the hosts of heaven and earth will pause to say 'Here lived a great street sweeper who did his job well."

Martin Luther King Jr.

My first job after college was not the most exciting. I believe my title was, "Data Entry Clerk Number 3" for a large company. To be honest, I don't even remember what the company's name was, or what they did. I sat at my desk in a cubicle and typed numbers from a huge stack of papers into a program on the computer. It was monotonous, tedious and boring. Those three words are probably not written on any job description/application anywhere. I didn't love the job, but I labored through it.

I had just graduated college, and was waiting to head off to Chiropractic school, so this job was a stop-gap. However, after a few weeks, I realized I really liked the people who worked there with me. They had much more exciting jobs than I did, it wasn't a room full of number-typer-inners (aka Data Entry Clerks). I enjoyed getting coffee at the community coffee machine (the coffee was actually really good). I enjoyed talking about football around the water cooler. I enjoyed having a taste of "real work life." In all honesty, I learned to appreciate the sense of calm the job provided. It was almost meditative. I would basically turn many portions of my brain off while I worked. You could say this was my first experience with meditation, even though at that point I had no clue about meditation or turning my mind off and enjoying stillness (more on mediation in a later chapter). I learned to take pride in small accomplishments/little victories through this job. I also received tremendous experience in working with other people. I definitely did not love the job itself, but I learned to love some aspects of it, and I know that it helped me grow as an individual and a worker. For that I'm grateful.

Joy can be found in any vocation. The key is to find what you love, or at least nuggets of love, that you can cultivate daily. And if what you're doing for your profession doesn't help stoke the fires of joy, then by all means it's IMPERATIVE you find a new job or position. Don't starve your soul. And, be honest, you know if you're joyful at work or if you ain't. I'm willing to bet others know as well.

Going through the motions just to bring a paycheck home is a slow death. In the meantime, you can definitely find SOME aspects of your job to focus on, that you enjoy. Focus on the good and stop complaining about the bad. Find things about your current position that you're grateful for. Funny thing about gratitude, when you give it some attention, it grows. You'll find that when you focus on the joy in your life, more things to be joyful about show up.

I don't know for sure, but I'm willing to bet that "slow-death" is not a profession listed for anyone, by any Guidance Counselor, anywhere.

The truth is, you are the true guide for YOUR life. You need to dig deep into your heart. Somewhere behind the valves, septum, ventricles and nodes there is an energy, a feeling, a love. And you know it's there too. You've felt it. You've sensed it. You've been with it. You've noticed how it flowed through your veins, how it nurtured your very existence. It may not be there full-bore at every waking moment, but you know it's there (and maybe there's also fear there, warning you to stay away, to say safe, to stay ...the same).

You've felt the spark when your favorite song comes on the radio. You've been warmed by it when cuddling with your sweetheart, or eating your favorite meal, or even sipping your favorite beverage. You've been lifted up by it when you laugh, or when you're in the company of your best friend(s). You are aglow when you're spending time connecting with family. That's joy. That's love. That's EVERYTHING.

You may find this feeling isn't attached to anything tangible at the moment. That's completely fine (and incredibly common). You may not be able to connect the dots of your joy to your vocation/creation/libation/imagination/whatever just yet, but you need to do some digging to find that spark.

If you don't love what you do right now, I'm sure you can find small pieces of your day that you do enjoy. The more you reach for that feeling, the more you cultivate it, the more it will come out to play and show up in your everyday life. It will help guide you toward your why, even if as of now, you have no idea at all what or where it is.

In order to connect what you do on a daily basis with your true joy for living, you are going to need to get to spelunking. Your true joy, your inspiration, may be buried deep under piles of papers, and suffocating under TPS reports (Insert *Office Space* reference here). It could be on page two-thirty-seven of that novel you keep telling yourself you're going to read. It could be hidden in a conversation you and your boss have yet to discuss. It could be found in a carpool that you haven't started taking part in. It could be sitting in the middle drawer of your desk, gently whispering for freedom. It doesn't matter how deep it may be. The good news is, once you've felt it, you know it exists, and you can find it again.

It's still there, yearning to get out. Start listening and start digging.

PURPOSELY POSITIVE EXERCISE: WHAT WOULD YOU DO

Grab your notebook and do the following:

- Answer this question:
  - What would you do with your life if you had an infinite amount of time and money?

- Anything. Anything at all. Don't think of any side-effects.

- There are no anchors in this exercise.

- Seriously, you're going to live forever, and you have a quadrillion-gazillion dollar allowance every 2 hours.

- Consider:

- What would you do, today?
- What about next week?
- Three years from now?
- What would you continually do?
- What would your soul still yearn to accomplish?
- What would you stop doing that you're doing right now?

WHY? WHY? WHY?

"You gotta have a WHY! You gotta have a reason for why you do what you do!"

—Eric Thomas

"Why? Why? Why?"

—Every three-year-old in the history of the
WORLD

I love Simon Sinek's book, and his amazing *ted.com* talk, *Start With Why: How Great Leaders Inspire Everyone to Take Action*[1] Simon discusses the core of purpose. He shares what he has dubbed, "The Golden Circle." Picture a target with three rings. The innermost ring is WHY. The second ring is HOW. The outer ring is WHAT. He points out that so many companies (and people) know their what (what they do), and sometimes their how (how they are different, how they do whatever it is they "do"), but few know WHY they do it, and if they do know their why, many times it's the lowest priority of the three.

He goes on to explain that we are totally working from the wrong side of the equation. Starting with WHY is genius. It's also

---

1. *https://www.ted.com/talks/simon_sinek_how_great_leaders_inspire_action*

exactly WHY people care, why they listen and why they buy what you're selling.

Your WHY is your spirit. Your WHY is your inspiration. Your WHY is your motivation. So, what's your why?

One of the best exercises I know to get to the root of this question is to pretend you are indeed a three-year-old and ask "why" over and over again until you get to the heart of it.

For example, if you say you want to be a gymnast...why? *Because you like the sport...why?* Because it is fun...why? *Because you love to exercise...why?* *You feel alive inside when you run and jump, and you feel beautiful as you soar through the air...* That's more like it. You love being a gymnast because it makes you feel alive.

Pretty solid answer, and a good foundation to start with (just so you don't get any ideas... I'm NOT a gymnast. I can do a somersault, kind of, but that's about it. My wife, however, was a gymnast and can create a balance beam out of any line, anywhere).

You have to know WHY you do what you do. Even more so, you need to know WHY you want to do anything. Even if you think you don't know why you have your current job, there is a WHY there. There's a reason you get out of bed every single morning (or evening, if that's your thing). Your current why may not be about saving the world or protecting ladybugs, but you have a why. It's in there somewhere. You have a reason (or many) that propels you from lying supine (face-up) on your bed, turning off the alarm (or maybe hitting snooze a couple of times, then turning it off), and heading downstairs (or upstairs, or inside, you may have some kind of amazing tree-house bedroom in the jungle) to begin your day.

Your why may still be in its infant form. It may be buried behind some false-hood or pretend whys, like "*I work to pay the bills*" or "*I have no other option*" or "*My mom made me get a job because I'm fifty-two and sleeping on her couch.*" Those are surface-based, "barely-whys." There is a deeper driving force that led you to your current situation/profession. It may take some digging and some, "why...why...why?" asking (until you are blue in the face), but you can and NEED to uncover the connection between what you're doing and WHY you're doing it. It is imperative to discover the connection between your why and the future you can create, when you uncover the deeper why, it will lead you to more opportunities, growth and amazement. When you find that why, it will undoubtedly propel you forward in all areas of your life.

Tony Robbins discusses six basic human needs and the idea of 'working' somehow actually being woven into quite a few of them.[2] He states that every human has a basic human need to feel unique and significant/needed.

As a human, you have a need to feel a connection with someone or something (or both). You have a need to grow/expand your capacity, capability or understanding, and a need to contribute, as in performing service and supporting others. Point being, work factors into quite a few of our basic needs. You have a basic need to work toward something, and as long as you connect the WHY of your soul to the WHAT that you do, you will be fulfilled.

Speaking of fulfilled, let's move onto the next chapter...

PURPOSELY POSITIVE EXERCISE: WORLD OF WHYS

Grab your notebook and do the following:

- Look back at what you wrote for the "what would you do if you could live forever and money was infinite" exercise—if you need to grab your notebook, I'll wait.

- Now pretend you're having a conversation with your three-year-old self, and "Little You" keeps asking "why" you would want to do the things you wrote down. Answer the question: why?

- And I mean answer it over and over again. Each time you answer, "Little You" keeps on pushing for a bigger/deeper explanation.

---

2. *https://www.tonyrobbins.com/mind-meaning/do-you-need-to-feel-significant/*

- You have to keep answering this guy/gal because after all, you're from the future and Little You deserves your candid answers.

- Keep answering the question "why" until you feel you've gotten to the root cause and the driving force for why you would do the things you wrote down.

MEANING...FULL

"Life is without meaning. You bring the meaning to it. The meaning of life is whatever you ascribe it to be. Being alive is the meaning."

—Joseph Campbell

"Challenging the meaning of life is the truest expression of the state of being human."

—Viktor E Frankl

You have a problem. As a human being, you seek happiness. You look to move toward pleasure and away from pain. That isn't a problem, that's just "normal." The problem (as I see it) is that your happiness lens can sometimes be skewed. For example, you can purchase and consume an infinite number of things to gather up some emotion that sparks what you would describe as happiness. That alone isn't a bad thing. It's that the cycle of these "grabs" is never-ending. You don't ever "get your fill." And you miss the biggest piece of the puzzle.

Things don't make you happy. The emotions tied to those things aren't sources of everlasting happiness, either. The biggest contributor to your happiness is your MEANING. What is your purpose? Why are you doing what you're doing right now? Your happiness is born and bred inside of your soul, and the seed is the meaning/purpose you attach to your actions, thoughts and circumstances of your daily life.

Viktor Frankl wrote a truly remarkable book: *Man's Search for Meaning*. It chronicles his time in a concentration camp during the Holocaust. There are quite a few books that breach that subject and do so very well. What made Frankl's stand out was that he was a neurologist and psychiatrist, and looked at his experiences through those lenses. He had a unique perspective: he observed his (and his co-captives) experiences from a scientific lens and could delve into why some lived through the atrocities, and why others did not.

What he found is that the vast majority of survivors had a strong sense of purpose. They had a life of meaning outside of their confined walls (and those less fortunate did not). The survivors had something to hold on to during their immense turmoil. Those who were able to find meaning in their suffering, or had a strong enough meaning to get through their suffering, fared far better than those who did not.

Think about a person standing in the middle of the road, and you see a bus approaching at high speed. What drives you to run into the road to save that person? It's the meaning you hold for that person. Maybe it's a relative. Maybe it's your wife. Maybe it's your child. Maybe it is a stranger and you just hold a love for the human race. Regardless of the exact reason, your meaning drives your action. Likewise, if it were you in the middle of the road, your meaning is what spurs you to move out of the way. This same sense of meaning is what causes you to get out of bed each morning and go on about your day. You want to have meaning in your life. You want to know that your time on this Earth is worth something and that you will be remembered when your time is up.

The meaning of your existence is one of the largest motivators to keep existing.

Many think that when they retire, they'll be living "the high life." Spending their retirement money, vacationing, golfing, and napping. Sounds great, doesn't it? But the truth is, studies show that retirement can boost your risk of depression by 40%. Additionally, the risk of being diagnosed with a "condition" increases by up to 60%.[1] That is not a small jump. Experts believe that a major factor of this is a lot of retired people have lost the connection to their purpose. They feel like they aren't contributing anymore. They question their meaning.

When you don't perceive your meaning, when you don't feel like you contribute, your very health declines. Further studies have shown that when retirees volunteer or find some way to contribute and to feel purposeful, their health improves again.

Although it is very similar to finding out why you do what you do, your *meaning* probes deeper. Your meaning pervades everything you do and every breath you take. You don't need to be 100% conscious of this meaning twenty-four hours a day, but if you can, investigate to find the root of it. Your meaning is vital...and it may change through time. You probably had a bit different meaning in the pre-parenthood phase of life and the always-tired (aka "parenthood") phase. Your meaning is allowed to evolve.

You may begin an adventure (or venture) with one meaning and through your experiences, that meaning changes shape; it pulls or pushes differently. Your meaning will change with life events. It can evolve through celebrations, marriages, divorces, deaths, big wins, big challenges. Your meaning will change shape from time-to-time, and that is completely acceptable. Which is why I believe it's monumentally beneficial to investigate and seek out this meaning continually, throughout your life. If you can get in touch with it and bring it to the forefront of your mind, your fuel for life will only grow.

This is especially important on tough days. When you can grab onto your meaning and have some cuddle-time with it, your mindset, your mentality, your focus, and your spirit will prosper.

Where to begin? Start with your core values. Your life has meaning because of the connection you have to your core values. The attitudes, thoughts, character traits you hold most dear are

---

1. Sahlgren, Gabriel *Work Longer, Live Healthier, Institute of Economic Affairs Discussion Paper Number 46, May 2013*

your core values. They are the principles and values that help you navigate how you live your life.

For example, you may value: a belief or disbelief in God, a belief that honesty is the best policy and integrity matters or a belief that family comes first in all things. Other values can include: loyalty, dependability, a good sense of humor, creativity, fitness, or patriotism. These are only a few possible examples of core values.

I don't know yours, as each person's are unique, but these values are the bedrock of your views on everything in life. They form the very surface that all your other thoughts, emotions, and actions are built upon. They are the flag that you plant firmly in the soil of your soul and use to act accordingly. You derive meaning in life by how closely your life and your dreams connect to these values. When you can define with solidarity the traits and feelings you hold most dear, and when you combine those with friendships, action, vocation, vacation, etc., you will find that your meaning in life is flourishing.

I suggest you take some time (it could take a while) to complete the PPE exercise because your life will be so much more meaningful if you do. These core values are the bedrock of your entire existence, and therefore set the stage for a solid future. It's hard to build a house when there's no foundation to speak of. If you don't believe me, just go ask two of the three little pigs.

If you need some further assistance with this (and who doesn't), there are some tremendous resources/exercises for finding meaning. Check out the Index of Inspiration at the end of this book.

PURPOSELY POSITIVE EXERCISE: DIGGING FOR CORE VALUES

Grab your notebook and do the following:

- What have you done in your life that you are most proud of? What are your greatest accomplishments?—write down three to five, at most (you're allowed to erase and start over).

- Consider: what makes these situations the greatest? What do they have in common?

- What do you consider your biggest failures in life so far?—write three to five of the biggest ones down.

- Consider: what do they have in common?

- Write some advice to yourself that would help you do more of Step 1 and less of Step 2—you can be wordy here—pretend you're actually having a conversation with "Little You" again.

- How would you summarize what "Big You" just told you?

- Make a cheatsheet of some of the conversation—can you summarize what to do more of and what to avoid in just a few words?

- List out the words that create more meaning in your life (and at the same time, stop you from going down the wrong path, losing meaning). For example: be joyful, love people more, and get into alignment.

- On another page make a list of the things you value—this is not about possessions, specifically, but more about your core values in life, such as happiness, health, abundance, love, etc.

- Take the time to highlight, circle, star, sticker, or emphasize the words that best represent the values you consider desirable, good, and worthwhile.

- Get the number of highlighted values down to five to seven—if you have more than that, take another pass, keep filtering down to get to the top five to seven that make the most sense and that you feel the most sure of today.

- Re-write these five to seven on a new page and then rank them from one to seven, with one being the most important—this could be hard. If you take the time to define what each value means to you, it may make it easier to rank them. By the way, this isn't an exact science, if you have a hard time ranking one and two as such, why not make a one-A and one-B?

- Consider: Why did you choose these values? Why are they important? How would following these values in your everyday life give you more meaning?

- Write out a sentence or two describing why these values relate to the meaning of your life

- Finally, Contact Monty Python, because that whole, *The Meaning of Life* movie doesn't hold a candle to what you just uncovered (those guys are hilarious though).

SHOW UP,
BE SEEN!

"We cultivate love when we allow our most vulnerable and powerful selves to be deeply seen and known, and when we honor the spiritual connection that grows from that offering with trust, respect, kindness and affection."

—BRENÉ BROWN

"To share your weakness is to make yourself vulnerable; to make yourself vulnerable is to show your strength."

—CRISS JAMI

There are instances in life where you just fit in. Things just feel right. You are where you're supposed to be when you're supposed to be there. However, all-too-often, you hide yourself. You hide your pieces. Why?

There are parts of you that you don't want the world to see.

Being truly vulnerable is a scary proposition. If everyone knew you, the "real" you, the whole you...what would they think? You don't want to find out, so you put on masks, even little ones. You conceal parts of yourself because you have judged them harshly and are afraid the world will feel the same. You keep these blemishes tucked away and out of sight. You play this crazy hide-and-*never*-seek game. Unfortunately, this game definitely doesn't have a happy ending, and if you're good at it, you end up playing it over and over again...alone.

You crave connection. In fact, you need it. Numerous studies have shown that one of the biggest indicators of happiness is the amount of quality connections, friendships, and relationships in your life. You need to have people to go through this crazy life with you. You need to feel part of something, and you need to feel that you are part of other people's lives. If you hold back parts of yourself, there is no way you can truly be connected.

Ever try to build a puzzle when you've purposely hidden four or five middle pieces? Not much fun when you are close to the end of putting that thing together. And let's just say you put the puzzle together anyway, and go to show it off to your friends (because who doesn't build a puzzle and then go door-to-door to demonstrate it's wonder?). Except they don't know what to make of it. Is it a zebra? Or a monkey on a broomstick? An M.C. Escher neverending staircase? Or something else? If you hold back some of the pieces, people will never get the whole picture, and they will never be able to revel in its awesomeness.

You may think the pieces you're keeping back are small or insignificant (or your inner voice has persuaded you to think they are), but they may end up being the cornerstones to the whole thing. You won't ever know. If you hide some of yourself, those you want to connect with fully won't know you completely, and you won't know them either.

In order to fulfill your soul's desire, and to leave a legacy in this world (because why else are you here), you have to be willing to stand up and be seen-every part of you. I will never forget, when my grandmother passed away. I was in high school. I was talking with my brother and we both (at first) discussed how we "needed to be strong" for our sisters, for our aunts and uncle and for our mom. We thought that "strong" meant "standing tall, not being sad, and not crying." Eventually, though, I realized that being strong wasn't about standing tall all the time. True strength was showing that we were hurting too, and that we were going to miss her. We needed to lean on others as well. After all, the strength of two people together is usually much stronger than that of the individual.

To quote Brené Brown once again: "Courage, the original definition of courage when it first came into the English language—it's from the Latin word cor, meaning heart —and the original definition was to tell the story of who you are with your whole heart...."[1]

I love that. For all you know about yourself, what could possibly be more courageous than letting the entire world see exactly who you are? When you play the coward and hide, when you sit even though you want to stand, when you don't raise your hand even though you know the answer, when you don't tell them you love them (and therefore they never say it back), when you fight back your tears (and therefore don't connect with the others who are in pain and could use some comfort), when you falsify integrity to try to be someone you are not, when you hold yourself back, you take more and more steps toward an unquestionably damaging state of affairs (and a sluggish existence).

Think back to a love-filled relationship you were a part of. You may have fallen fast and hard, but I'd be willing to wager that the love hit its peak and you BOTH felt the best in the relationship when you experienced unbridled connection. When your souls were entwined, when you were walking a path together (both of you).

Call to mind your best friend. I bet you didn't just decide she was on the top of your friend list (and maybe even the person you gave half of your awesome BFF locket to) because she enjoyed N'SYNC or Bon Jovi or Five Finger Death Punch as much as you did. I doubt she is your best friend because she gave you stuff, or because she helped you cheat on your math test. You chose her (consciously or unconsciously) because you were kindred spirits. You laughed together, had fun together, and cried together. You could truly BE YOU around them.

Love and true friendship have one huge thing in common: vulnerability. You let down your guard. You let the other person see

---

1. *https://www.ted.com/talks/brene_brown_on_vulnerability*

you a bit more than the rest of the world sees you. It feels great to know you don't need to stash some of yourself away. And here's the funny thing—you LIKE YOURSELF more when you're around the people you care about. They make you feel good. They make you comfortable. They make you feel whole. They play a role in that, most assuredly, but a huge portion of that feeling comes from the fact that you are "being whole" around them. You're sharing all of who you are (or at least more of yourself than you would normally). You're grounded. You're loved. You're understood and you're connected.

What if you cultivated that feeling more often in your day-to-day life? You don't have to run out into the world stark naked yelling, "Here I am Mount Pleasant, Indiana! I am truly vulnerable!" I mean, you can if you want, but that's not what I'm trying to allude to (and just for the record, I will not pay your public indecency ticket if you choose to go that route). You can bring more of yourself to your everyday life, though. You can laugh, feel sad, scared, blessed, grateful or worried. You can let your feelings and your personality show. You can dare to be the first to say those three words. You can be the first to ask for help and the first to offer it; you can be willing to follow where your soul is longing for you to go. You can have the courage to accept the fact that you may have flaws, but you're whole. You can choose to unveil yourself, to be noticed, to be acknowledged, and to shout to yourself and to the world: I AM ENOUGH! And that's the whole truth and nothing but the truth!

PURPOSELY POSITIVE EXERCISE: WHOLE-SOME

Grab your notebook and write down the following:

- Who makes you feel whole?
- Who are you most comfortable around?
- Describe these people in as much detail as you can.

- What activities do you do with them?

- What do you both enjoy?

- Why do you feel so at ease around them?

- What do they bring out in you that you hide (consciously or subconsciously) around others?

CONSTANT CHANGE

"He who rejects change is the architect of decay. The only human institution which rejects progress is the cemetery."

—HAROLD WILSON

"The great tragedy of life is often not in our failure, but rather in our complacency; not in our doing too much, but rather in doing too little; not in our living above our ability, but rather in our living below our capacities."

—BENJAMIN E. MAYS

Change is the only constant in life. A smart man named Heraclitus said something quite similar to that a few years back (somewhere between 535 B.C. and 475 B.C.). *"There is nothing permanent, except change."* Things have changed a bit since then (see what I did there?), but the truth remains: almost everything is changing, all around us, constantly. It's easy to notice this with the change of seasons (unless you live along the equator where the seasons are pretty much the same, then you might not have a concept of what I am talking about). As time passes, everything on this Earth is transforming. The grass you stand on today is not the same grass you stood on last year. The air you are breathing today is different than what you breathed yesterday. I hope what you're having for lunch is different than what you've had every day for the past few months. You are not who you were last year, let alone thirty years ago. So don't let your past define your future. You couldn't really do that even if you tried.

Living off your accomplishments from the past may get you a bit ahead in the here and now, but not for very long. And hiding who you can become due to some mistakes you might have made in the past is just as idiotic and worthless. Pride and regret are the parents of lethargy. If you want to have a pulse, you're going to need to accept that change is happening, and it's happening at this very moment.

Take your amazing body, for example. Red blood cells have about a four-month lifespan. The cells that line your trachea live for about one to two months; the lining of your small intestine for two to four days. The lining of your stomach for two to nine days. Your fat cells...eight years (I know. I was hoping we could kill those guys off a bit quicker). All these cells inside your body are constantly changing and reforming, over and over again. One other interesting thing about this short list you just read... the more possible "trauma" to the cells, usually the faster the turnaround and the faster the growth. Isn't that interesting?

Growth is necessary for survival. If you aren't expanding your horizons, you're slowly dying. Growth happens quicker the more trauma you feel and the more you experience challenges. So don't shy away from opportunities to grow. Challenges are usually doors to a brighter future. Now I'm not saying go "traumatize" yourself on purpose. Diving head first into a pool without water will definitely cause some challenges, but not the kind I'm thinking of. I'm saying the true masterminds, the successes, the outliers and the high performers in life, have learned to look for the opportunities hidden inside the challenges. They don't just "roll with the punches" of change. They use those punches to propel them into something greater.

If you are willing to accept from the evidence previously presented (just re-read a couple paragraphs higher on the page for a refresher)—that change is always happening—then you must realize these changes can be perceived as positive or negative. You're going to experience troubles and exhilarations, that is the plain and simple truth. When the victories come, celebrate, and plan on the next one. When the knock downs happen, don't let them keep you there. Realize that within these traumas lies the opportunity to grow at an even faster rate. You learn more from episodes viewed as losses than from the "wins." So when you are getting your butt kicked in life, take a moment to just think: "OK, so this is crappy. But I know from the science of intestinal cell turnover that I will grow from this experience quicker than I would have had I not gone through this crap-storm."

So, what are you going to learn from this change? How can you let this experience propel you more toward the person you want to be?"

· On the other side of the "what's going on in your life" coin—things could be fantastic. I truly hope things are the best they've ever been in your life. Truly, I do. But it's my job to tell you this... things won't always be that way.

I'm not saying eventually the other shoe will drop (I never really understood the significance of that phrase... why in the hell would anyone be fearful of a shoe falling? Where would it be falling from? And why do they have only one shoe?). What I am saying is that things will indeed change. No matter where things are right now, it's an absolute certainty that they won't always be this way. They may be better, they may be worse, but they won't just BE. Complacency guarantees a down-hill slide. Always playing it safe is the exact same as not playing at all. Complacency breeds boredom. Boredom is the opposite of inspired.

A positive, vibrant, inspiring life cannot be attained through complacency. It requires change.

Lou Holtz, a wildly successful former Notre Dame football coach, has been quoted as saying *"If what you did yesterday seems big, you haven't done anything today."* Due to the inarguable certainty that things change, you cannot rest on past accomplishments. By the very nature of nature itself, unless you are progressing, you are failing. I'm not saying you need to stockpile success after success (that isn't the way the world works, either), but if you are sedentary in your aims, if you rest for too long, if you don't accept that you need to change along with the world, you will go absolutely nowhere (but at least you will travel with caution), and the trophies you've earned up until this moment will look great in your cabinet but will wither and become rusted relics with time.

Don't give up trying, even if you think you've "made it." There really isn't a difference between the person who never begins and the person who sits back on their past successes: both people are still just sitting.

Learn. Explore. Try. Experiment. Veer. Attempt. Dabble. Break habits. Form new ones. You might just like the person you become even more than who you were before…

PURPOSELY POSITIVE EXERCISE: WHATCHA WANNA DO?

Grab your notebook and do the following:

- Write down something that you'd love to improve on—have you ever wanted to learn to play the Ukulele?

- Wondered how to crochet?

- Desired to dabble in Japanese Calligraphy?

- Do you want to improve your tiramisu-baking game?

- Consider: What is a "hobby" you've always thought "looks interesting," but you've never looked into it more than that? (I can almost guarantee there's an app for that.)

- Go do the thing you wrote down—give yourself the gift of change. In today's world, there are countless ways to learn something new, or to improve a skill you have a hankering to be better at.

TETHERED MIND

*"Concentrate all your thoughts upon the work at hand.
The sun's rays do not burn until brought to a focus."*

—ALEXANDER GRAHAM BELL

So, no offense...but you kind of have the mind of a monkey. "Monkey mind" is a Buddhist term meaning "unsettled, restless, inconsistent and confused." Basically, the term describes what you do when you bounce from thought-to-thought, and action-to-action, and are not able to sit and concentrate on one thing at a time. However, as a society, we have taken pride in the ability to "muti-task."

For the record: "multi-tasking" is NOT a redeeming quality. It is FAR better to concentrate on one task and to complete it with 100% focus than to try and juggle many things and complete each one at 40% to 50%. "Research shows that the brain doesn't really do tasks simultaneously, as we thought (hoped). Each time you move from hearing music to writing a text or talking to someone, there is a stop/start process that goes on in the brain."[1]

In today's fast-paced, results-now world, our monkey minds are extremely well-fed. Our minds are a battlefield and the war wages on. You are bombarded by stimuli every few waking seconds. The

---

1. *https://www.psychologytoday.com/blog/creativity-without-borders/201405/the-myth-multitasking.*

average hour long TV show is composed of 35% to 41% commercials.[2] The average song on the radio is about three minutes. Every quarter, kickoff, field goal, and probably fumble in a football game is "brought to you" by someone. You have a lot of information to take in, and your brain is exceptionally good at doing so. The speed of nerve impulses to and from the brain can be as high as one hundred meters (0.06 mile) per second. This "slows" to twenty to thirty meters per second if you give the impulse some deep thought.

When you look at these statistics, is it any wonder that your monkey mind thrives and drastically overrules your calm, contemplative, fully-present side? There is a time and a place to let these monkeys loose, to let them bounce around, to use them to figure out the solution to a problem, to let them expend some built-up energy.

The issue is that you have been trained (more and more in modern life) to let the monkeys rule the forest. That is NOT the way it should work. The mind-monkeys play a vital role in your life. You need the mind-monkey to process all the information you receive on a daily basis and be able to catch a percentage of it. But you don't need to feed the monkeys a never-ending buffet. As stated earlier, they are already fed—without any help—all day long.

What you need to do is to give some attention to calming the monkeys and, therefore, fostering some peace in your mind.

So how do you get these monkeys to stop bouncing around all the time? It isn't a matter of changing them, it's a matter of devoting some time and energy into being calm, being present, being here and now.

Step one is simple. You're already doing it but not *noticing* it. Breathe. Just stop a couple times a day and notice your breath. When I first started this practice, and reading about being mindful using meditation, I attacked it. I tried to wrestle my monkeys and force my mind to be calm and present. Needless to say, that didn't end too well for me. I tried to "win" at being present. I remember a conversation I had with a great friend and mentor, Dr. Dennis

---

2. *http://www.marketingcharts.com/television/primetime-tv-hour-includes-41-commercials-9434/*

James. I told him, "I'm working hard on just allowing life more this year and focusing on being present." His response? "*Well, grasshopper...*" just kidding (he doesn't talk like that). What he actually said, was, "*Joel, you can't really WORK on ALLOWING. Those are basically opposite words.*"

He made an excellent point. I did need to make an effort to include "allowing" (being present, mindful, etc.) in my routine, but the truth was, I really needed to *let go* in order to be mindful. There is an excellent book on this subject and the tribulations involved in working toward mindfulness and mediation. Dan Harris, co-anchor of *Nightline* and the weekend edition of *Good Morning America*, wrote about his experiences in this realm. The book is called, "*10% Happier: How I Tamed the Voice in My Head, Reduced Stress Without Losing My Edge, and Found Self-Help That Actually Works—A True Story,*" and it is surely worth a read. In it he discusses having the same trouble I was having: getting so frustrated that I couldn't be "present" during meditation. It's very common: you close your eyes and listen to some dulcet-toned instructor telling you to empty your mind and just breathe. But then your subconscious starts blasting you with random thoughts about bills you need to pay, the juice you need to buy from the grocery store, or the weird kid who sat next to you in the second grade who could never stop picking his nose. You get frustrated because you can't just turn that subconscious off. And then low-and-behold, the conscious and subconscious are on full throttle. So much for clearing your mind!

Later on my journey into meditation, I learned that the key wasn't trying to clear my mind completely. The subconscious will always be wanting to get its word in edgewise. I just needed to acknowledge some of those monkey-mind thoughts and move on, not push them away with vigor. Allowing those thoughts to be heard but not worked through was the key to remaining still. If a thought pops in your mind, you say "thanks for that thought, I'll get back to you later." Calming the monkey-mind is about learning to be still and bringing some tranquility into your busy life.

Improving yourself can be hard work. But you also need to know when to ALLOW change to happen and when to just be O.K. with how things are at the moment. I know it's a conundrum. When you're working on yourself, it's easy to push and push and push, and never allow for recovery. Even gigantic bodybuilders know they can't work out hard seven days a week and expect progress to be made. If they push that hard on a consistent basis, they will actually lose muscle, rather than gain it. They need at least one day of "recovery" (many people flip that equation too often: one day of exercise, six days of recovery). The same rule applies here. You should work on yourself, but also know that part of the work is taking time to rest occasionally. Your soul needs time for the changes you've made to manifest and take shape.

Sometimes, accepting the day for what it is, is actually the very best way to improve the world. Don't demean it. Don't try to improve it. Don't try to insert your will upon it, because on certain days, if you try to change it, you negate the beauty of what it means to be a soul having a human experience. Sometimes the very best way to improve your life in the moment is to simply accept your joy. Only improve upon that which you can improve upon (you can quote me on that one!).

If you go out into the world destined to improve it for everyone, that is a truly noble and amazing purpose. But what happens when you just want to enjoy Saturday for Saturday's sake? Your purpose needs to be so strong that you are O.K. with letting up some slack every now and then. Sunsets are amazing. Can you add to them? Sure, you may be able to enjoy the moment more fully by sharing it with someone you love. The beauty may inspire thoughts that uplift you even more, but you cannot make God's gift of a sunset more beautiful than it already is. You don't have that power, and quite honestly, you probably wouldn't want it. Breathe it in and savor. Sometimes the simple act of a breath is magic in itself. You have to let go sometimes, and just let things BE. (On a side note, I highly recommend a few apps for this. Check out the Breathe App through the iTunes store. It gives you daily reminders and practice to just focus on breathing for one minute at a time. Also, Insight Timer is a great meditation app for beginners and gurus alike. Check them out, you won't be disappointed).

It is vital to put your monkey-mind to rest on occasion in order to improve your ability to make the world a more positively serene place.

"...*and his effect was tranquility.*" That is the end of a sentence in *From The Corner of His Eye*, a Dean Koontz novel. (You can connect to inspiration in the most unexpected places). What a great sentence. When you work on calming your own monkey mind, you also can have the power to be a source of tranquility for others. Again, don't go too far and think you need to become the flowy-robed guru; just realize that everyone you bump into is also living in a chaotic state. The Autonomic Nervous System has two dominant parts: sympathetic and parasympathetic. The parasympathetic portion is the calm side, working under the radar: calm heart, calm min, and calm breath system.

The sympathetic portion is often referred to as the "fight or flight" side. Most people are veering more and more away from parasympathetic dominance and into sympathetic dominance. This is a problem because on a day-to-day basis, you really don't need to fight things or flight (run) from things. Your monkey-mind is still trained to kick things into high gear though. So if you can work on bringing some more calm into your own life, and tip the scales back to a more neutral place between the sympathetic and parasympathetic nervous system, it will undoubtedly expand into the realm of helping others as well. When you can calm your own chaos, you are helping others with theirs.

As you continue on your journey of self-discovery, reaching toward your inspiration and allowing it to turn the tide from negative to positive, realize that sometimes you just need to sit back, breathe, and notice. Pausing in your busy life for moments at a time can help calm your monkeys, improve focus, and allow (ironically) for more time to get things done. Relaxing a bit (on purpose) will lower your stress levels, improve circulation, and benfit your overall physical and mental health.

Sounds like a pretty good cost-to-benefit ratio to me. Taking some time to relax and to be calm is a vital cog in your transformation.

PURPOSELY POSITIVE EXERCISE: WHOLE LOTTA NOTHIN'

Do the following:

- Tonight (or tomorrow morning), pour yourself your favorite beverage, sit in a comfy chair outside, and leave your phone (and smartwatch—that counts too) inside.

- Grab a blanket if needed, or a cool rag for your head if it's the opposite end of the temperature spectrum where you live.

- Sit. Relax. Revel—don't write and try not to think of too many other things.

- Observe for fifteen minutes (or so).

- Breathe.

- Take in what you see.

- Notice—imbibe the beauty.

- Isn't that nice?

- After the fifteen minutes are up, stop and notice how much better you truly feel

- Incorporate the gift of stillness into your life for a few minutes every day.

STRUGGLE-RIFIC

"Strength and growth come only through continuous effort and struggle."

—Napoleon Hill

"I always say, dare to struggle, dare to grin."

—Wavy Gravy

How many times have you found yourself slogging through your life, pushing through your day at work, jumping over hurdles and thinking, "Why can't this just end?!" No doubt you have had moments where you were caught in desperation asking for a reprieve. Struggle. It's part of life. Don't take the trials you face for granted because on the other side of struggle lies progress. You CANNOT have one without the other.

You're going to face challenges. You're going to fall on your face one time or a hundred times. In your life, people are going to turn away from you. You will grasp at air sometimes when reaching for a hand. You will come up short and you're going to hear "no." From time-to-time your story will be grief and loss and denial and betrayal and sadness (boy, what an uplifting book this is!). Life is rife with disappointments. But that doesn't mean you get to let them rule. For each of these emotions, there is an exact opposite, and you wouldn't truly know beauty unless the negatives exist. Contrast is necessary.

On your journey to becoming and living your best self, you will get slapped with a tremendous amount of challenges, varying in their scope and depth. Strength, freedom, and joy are gained on the other side of these challenges. Every single inspirational figure in the annals of history forged his or her legacy due to some form of struggle. I have yet to read a story about someone who woke up, was gifted with amazing talent, and strolled through life, and brought love and freedom to the masses, without any setbacks, failures, or hardships. That just isn't the way this world works, and would be an absolutely awful book.

If you look back on your own life and think of some of your biggest wins, I bet there was a feeling of loss or a fail somewhere along the way. As with any emotion, you get to decide what purpose the feeling will serve in your life. You can look back on so many "success stories" and gain insight into the recurring theme of struggle.

Henry Ford's (you may have heard of the car company) first company, The Detroit Automobile Company, went out of business in 1901. The Henry Ford Company founded later was also abandoned, and his third company almost failed due to low sales.

KFC's "secret" recipe was almost kept a secret. Harland David Sanders (aka "the Colonel") had more than one thousand rejections before a restaurant finally agreed to work with him.

Oprah Winfrey was fired from her job as a television reporter because they felt she was "unfit for TV."

Steven Spielberg was rejected from the University of Southern California School of Theater, Film and Television three times.

Jack London (author of *White Fang* and *The Call of the Wild*) was rejected six-hundred times before his first story was published.

Michael Jordan (you may have heard of his shoes) was cut from his high school basketball team.

Stephen King was rejected thirty times when he tried to publish his novel, *Carrie*. He actually threw the book into the trash, and his wife fished it out and encouraged him to resubmit it.

Walt Disney was once fired from a newspaper because he "lacked imagination and had no good ideas." He also started (and failed) at a number of businesses.

Thomas Edison was told he was stupid as a child and couldn't learn anything. He made one thousand unsuccessful attempts at inventing the light bulb before gaining his success.

Fred Astaire was regarded quite poorly by the testing director of MGM at his first screen test. The director said of Astaire: "Can't act. Can't sing. Can dance a little."

Harrison Ford (Han Solo, *Indiana Jones*, *The Fugitive*) was told in his first film by the film's executives that he just didn't have what it took to be a star.

Elvis Presley (you may have seen his dance moves) was told by a manager of the Grand Ole Opry (after firing him based on one performance): "You ain't going nowhere son. You ought to go back to drivin' a truck."

The list could go on for another hundred pages or so. If you want to find an inspiring story that details overcoming struggle, you need not look very hard. As Author, Brendon Burchard puts it, "Let us remember that humanity's story has only two perennially recurring themes: struggle and progress."[1] That is undeniable truth. In order for progress to take place, there must be some form of prior struggle.

The good news is that the struggle doesn't have to be directly proportional to the success.

That fact, I believe, hinders a lot of people. If you achieve something with what seems like a small amount of difficulty, it doesn't negate the achievement. Likewise, if you achieve a small victory after getting pummeled for quite some time, it doesn't lessen the fact that it was a victory. People also fall into the mistake of thinking that unless they dealt with ginormous problems—as they have read about so many times—their successes won't be as ginormous either. They aren't one in the same. You don't need to come from an exceptionally horrible, tenuous background in order to live an

---

1. Burchard, Brendon. *The Motivation Manifesto*: Carlsbad, CA: Hay House Publishing, 2014. Print

amazingly inspired life. Those stories are awesome to hear about for sure, but all that truly matters is the end result. People sometimes trick themselves into believing they need to be starving in order to be an artist. While a lot can be attained through deep turmoil, you needn't go looking for it in order to persuade yourself that you can become a success. The hindrances will come, no sense in seeking them out. You will face challenges, and the scope of those challenges will vary in depth and character. Don't make the fatal mistake of thinking that the severity of the challenge equals the spirit of the success.

You just need to accept the fact that struggles are never going to be eradicated (until you cease to breathe). You shouldn't aim to get rid of them. I was talking (actually, texting, it's 2018) with a friend and colleague the other day about "slipping and checking." It's a phrase that basically means while on the path of transformation, you will slip or you will get a gut-check, or something of the sort will show you that you were "off." Then you can have a chance to "re-right" the ship. He said (again, 'texted') something to the tune of, "I can't wait until I don't slip anymore." My response was: "That's never gonna happen." I went on to say that the key isn't slipping less, or not slipping at all, it's *realizing* you've slipped quicker and quicker, and re-aligning your sails faster and faster. It's about stumbling, but catching yourself before you face-plant into the mud. It's completely normal to slip, just as long as you "check yourself" before you "wreck yourself" (Ice Cube said so). Struggles provide opportunity for growth, rather than for failure.

Re-frame your outlook on challenges. In the book, *The Book of Joy*, by Douglas Abrams, the Dalai Lama and Archbishop Desmond Tutu are interviewed on the topic of joy. At one point in the book, the author discusses research conducted by Pathik Wadhwa. The research concluded that stress and opposition during fetal development are exactly what initiate the developmental process in utero. Basically, without some stress in the womb, stem cells do not differentiate; they do not proliferate; they do not start the all-important process of becoming you. When you were just a couple cells, hardship/struggle was necessary to grow.

If you can look at your hardships as challenges, it allows for you to view them as opportunities or springboard points. Every diving board dips some before it propels you. When you view your challenges as the "dip before the launch" (again, the dip and the launch are not necessarily of the same magnitude), you will realize there are learning opportunities in every perceived negative situation.

For example, what can you do differently? What can you protect yourself from? What can you dive deeper into? What can you say/do next time? Is there a little 'tweak' you could initiate to lessen the chance of this happening again? What door is opening now that this one has closed? These type of questions will help ensure that the exact same slip doesn't happen again, and when a similar hurdle presents itself, at least you have "seen this road before" and can take steps to get back to where you want to be to clear the hurdles sooner rather than later.

PURPOSELY POSITIVE EXERCISE: FACE-PLANT TO GREATNESS

Grab your notebook and do the following:

- Recall a time that you failed

- Not just a slip, but a failure.

- It doesn't have to be a huge thing, although it can be. Did you:

  ○ Wreck a Jeep Wrangler?

  ○ Destroy a Dutch Oven?

  ○ Fuego up a friendship?

- Just bring to mind a time that you consider a slip.

- Write down: What has happened in your life (on the positive end of the spectrum) that may not have happened if you never made that mistake?

- I bet you won't have to look too hard, and even if you do, that's O.K. Look harder.

- There is always a positive on the other side of negative.

"UGGGGGHHHHH...
NOYANCES"

*"I don't have pet peeves like some people. I have whole ker-
nels of irritation."*

—WHOOPI GOLDBERG

*"Be master of your petty annoyances and conserve your en-
ergies for the big, worthwhile things. It isn't the mountain
ahead that wears you out—it's the grain of sand in your
shoe."*

—MARQUIS DE CUSTINE

Have you ever noticed how many times you can lose your cool
over the smallest things? You spill a little coffee on your
shirt, you notice your spouse forgets to buy milk (and she was already at the grocery store), or you have to do that crazy toothpaste
smoothing/roll-up origami to squeeze the last drop out so your
breath doesn't offend everyone in the morning. There is no possible way anyone could look at these things as life-shattering. But in
the moment, you act AS IF they are.

You can begin your day with great intentions, checklists, surely
ready to take on the world, and then something small happens and
suddenly you get derailed. In his book, *Triggers: Creating Behavior
That Lasts—Becoming The Person You Want To Be,* author, Mar-

shall Goldsmith, discusses how there is a definite difference between the planner and doer in your own mind. He also makes a great point that sometimes the littlest of things can knock your internal doer off the track. He calls these little instances "life's papercuts." What a brilliant analogy! Paper cuts definitely won't kill you, but they're so dang annoying, and in all honesty, they hurt... like hell! Run your finger over a piece of paper and feel a searing inferno of pain (maybe I'm a wimp, but go with me here.) You drop the paper (and probably your coffee) and then yell some sort of expletive, and you immediately assess the damage, expecting to see a large gash or a severed limb. Instead you find a little teensy-weensy sliver. Sometimes you even squeeze it until it bleeds a little, so you don't feel like such a baby. The point is, the damage does not equal the sensation. Sound familiar?

In life, these slight instances can create an explosion on perfectly laid plans. The planner in you sets the stage for a beautiful, Namaste-ish day. You sing happy songs in the car, drink your Get Happy, Be Happy Tea (they are actually real products made by The Republic of Tea; I totally bought some right after typing this sentence), roll the windows down to appreciate the beauty of the world around you– and then you get stuck in bumper-to-bumper traffic for who-knows-what-reason. And suddenly your oxytocin/serotonin/happiness cocktail gets drowned out by a flush of cortisol. You feel and act as if this twenty-minute traffic delay is going to ravage your entire day. Your entire physiology changes, and it isn't pretty.

It isn't just traffic either. People who chew loudly, people who talk loudly on their cell phone in public, a slowdown in internet speeds, your partner/spouse not replacing the toilet paper roll when it's empty, the rear-view camera not showing on the screen when the car is in reverse, application forms don't have enough space to write the answer, tangled headphone wire, pen clicking, the list of "pet-peeves" could go on forever. Do a simple internet search and you will find hundreds of these small things that are, in reality, quite silly, but can send normal people through the roof and make them go completely bonkers (FYI: there is some scientific reasons for why these things bother you so much. Sometimes they trigger responses in your brain that mimic responses to things far more egregious. Often, you are programmed to a higher sensitivity to things. But most times, you just plain overreact).

The derailment doesn't always begin with other people either. Ever had a day that was going great until you, for example, clip your side view mirror as you back your car out of the garage? You get a flat tire when you're heading to work. Your pants get caught in the door as you are trying to get into your car. There's a huge list of things that could "go wrong" between getting out of bed and driving to work. These things can all take place in the first hour or two of your day. Then you find yourself saying, "And the day just went downhill from there."

I've always hated when people leave their shopping carts sitting abandoned in a parking lot. Or when they do that little "prop the front end up on a curb" thing rather than walking the cart back to one of the ten cart return areas scattered throughout the lot. As comedian, Kellen Erskine puts it, "You're telling me you can meander two and a half miles inside Costco and the moment you get to your vehicle, you are like: not another step!" When I witness these forsaken carts on my weekly grocery store run, it would always irk me severely. My amazing wife has had to hear me rant numerous times about common decency and caring for one's fellow man and "these dang kids today!" I'm sure she just tuned me out after a while. My blood pressure would rise, the vein in my forehead would pulsate, and I would succeed at giving myself a headache. One day, however, I noticed a woman walking with a cane. She had just finished loading her purchases into her van and then was helping her handicapped child into the back seat. I'm sure her trip around the grocery store was a more arduous experience than mine was. I never realized that some of these abandoned carts could be connected to such narratives. Now when I get frustrated at the solitary carts in the parking lot at my local grocery store (it still happens), I can decide to stop and think about a possible legitimate story connected to them. Many times, I'm sure the story is that the person was just lazy, but I still get to choose my reaction.

The good news is you get to decide how you act (and react) when these instances occur. There is a split-second moment in time between the THING happening and your REACTION. You can learn to pause, interpret, choose a response from the list in your head (there are always multiple choices), and then react. You don't have to be a creature of impulse. You have too large of brain for that.

Step one is really simple: breathe. I'm pretty sure you remember how to do that. Just pause, draw in a long breath, and then exhale slowly. Maybe even do it a couple of times. That alone will drain a bit of the cortisol that was rising a second ago.

Next, consider the actual ramifications of the issue (not the super-inflated, knee-jerk reaction of the apocalypse-will come-if-I'm-ten-minutes-late scenario). Chances are, the actual is much less tragic than the imagined.

And finally, choose how you want to react. There may be times that you truly want to just get ticked off. More power to you, but 99.567% of the time, you will realize you don't want to be mad. You can chillax a bit and realize you have more time to sip your Happy Tea, and listen to more songs on your Happy Days playlist, and all will be right with the world again soon. The little annoyances that happen in your day-to-day (and they will happen) can knock you right off your path of purpose, but it's your choice whether or not you let it.

In this journey of transformation, don't let the paper-cuts bleed you dry.

PURPOSELY POSITIVE EXERCISE: STORY TIME

Have you ever read: *Alexander and the Terrible, Horrible, No Good, Very Bad Day*, by Judith Viorst? Alexander wakes up with gum in his hair (he went to sleep with gum in his mouth the night before) and then the rest of the day just seems to get worse and worse. Even small circumstances seem to be synonyms for awful.

Grab your notebook and do the following:

- Have some fun writing your own version of the *Alexander* book—describe

- A day full of tiny instances that can make your day seem horrible. (It doesn't need to be gum in the hair.)

- Make sure it applies to your current life and age.

- Describe all the awful things that happen on your very bad day.

- Then at the end, make sure you describe how good laying in your bed feels, how comfortable you are in the evening.

- Write down how excited you are that the day is over and fresh start is beginning tomorrow.

- Describe how wonderful it is to realize that even such a horrible day doesn't change your future for the worst.

EMINEMPATHY

"You'd have to walk a thousand miles in my shoes just to see what it's like to be me."

—EMINEM (MARSHALL MATHERS III)

"Empathy is the most mysterious transaction that the human soul can have, and it's accessible to all of us, but we have to give ourselves the opportunity to identify, to plunge ourselves in a story where we see the world from the bottom up or through another's eyes or heart."

—SUE MONK KIDD

So I admit it: I'm kind of an Eminem fan. I don't idolize him, I just like almost all genres of music, and his beats and lyrics get me energized and ready to take on the day. (If you've ever seen *Office Space*, the character at the beginning was totally me in high school and college, I had a Hyundai Excel that had two gigantic speakers in the back through which mostly loud bass-heavy music poured out. Of course, I made sure to turn the music down at stoplights and in neighborhoods).

Eminem is a lyricist. He has a way of pulling emotions out from his soul and putting them onto paper and into his songs. He can also freestyle and rap really, really fast. In many songs, he's quite angry. Those aren't my favorite. But one theme is fairly common among many of his tracks: empathy. He discusses how no one can truly know what his life is like unless they walked in his shoes. He talks about his critics often and how they're mainly just throwing darts because they don't have a clue what he goes through. I think this is spot-on and can apply to everyone in life.

Empathy is defined as the ability to understand and share the feelings of another. Seems simple enough, except that it isn't. You have your own struggles and your own victories to attend to. You have challenges and your own comforts. Fact: you will never truly know what it's like to be someone else, nor can he know what it's like to be you. But you need not go into battle like Eminem does in his music. Don't shout to the world, "You have no idea what my life is like you (insert expletive here) critics, so back off!" I believe what you need to do is to accept that no one can truly understand you because he *ain't* you. And because of his lack of understanding, you need to be better about letting things go.

The last chapter went over various pet-peeves and I won't re-name them here. However, many of them are created through the actions of others: a person cuts you off in traffic, a lane opens up in the grocery store and the people behind you in line jump over to it instead of allowing you to go in front, a guy walks in a door right in front of you and just lets it close without holding it for you, etc.

If you look hard enough, there are countless opportunities for you to feel slighted or disrespected. *"Don't they know what I am going through? I'm a person too. They should empathize with me more."* Now, does that make any sense at all? You have no control over the lives of others. Empathy cannot be enforced. You can't make others understand you, especially in short fragments of time.

What you can do is flip the switch. You can control your emotions. You can selectively choose which thoughts to follow and which path to take in your actions.

If you truly want to be the best version of you, start by having compassion toward others on a grander scale (which, ironically, begins with small steps and bigger thoughts). What if you stopped for a second at that first sign of anger toward another and just contemplated the possibilities of her day? She could've just found out her company is downsizing. Her mom could be very ill. She could be late to get to her child's doctor's appointment. She could have a family emergency. The possibilities are endless (and, yes, she could just be a total jerk, but the percentages of the she is Queen Jerk instances are much smaller than the she's a normal, non-jerk scenarios. And even if she is a jerk, you aren't going to change her jerkhood by being angry, slighted or annoyed).

You make snap decisions during initial swells of emotion when in truth, you are completely ignorant of the motives behind the other person's actions.

By the way, the feelings you get in these situations are completely natural, I'm not saying you're a horrible person for having them. I'm saying that, just like any other situation, there is a possibility for growth and learning. If you choose to step back for a minute, and practice empathy (and not foolishly think you can enforce it on others), the circumstance will surely be improved. You'll lower your blood pressure, improve your outlook, and set the stage for a greater day/week/month/life.

Take the time to pause and think about all lives besides just your own. Every person on this Earth is living his or her own life, and you have no idea what that means for each individual. When you feel slighted, chill out. Realize others probably didn't do it on purpose. After all, he or she is walking different miles than you are, and in completely different shoes.

PURPOSELY POSITIVE EXERCISE: SCENARIO SORCERY

- Imagine the following scenario: You are in a huge hurry driving to the local shopping center because you need to get last minute supplies for your all-important presentation to the board. And then...

  ○ A mini-van cuts you off in traffic—twice!

  ○ As you're pulling into the parking lot, the same van speeds in front of you and steals your parking spot.

- ∘ You are not happy with Maniacal-Minivan-Mom, Molly.

- ∘ You roll your window down, ready to tell Ms. Molly what you think of her when you notice....

- Fill in the blank. Describe the scene.

- It turns out she had GREAT reasons to be in even more of a hurry than you.
  - ∘ What are they?

- Maybe she even starts a conversation with you, after apologizing for her driving behavior and explains the whole bit. How does her story go?

- Consider: What can you learn from this experience?

"TIME...IS ON MY SIDE, YES IT IS?"

"The greatest obstacle to living is expectancy, which hangs upon tomorrow and loses today. You are arranging what lies in Fortune's control and abandoning what lies in yours."

—Seneca: On The Shortness of Life; Life is Long if you Know How to Use It

"Lost time is never found again."

—Benjamin Franklin

Eighty-six-thousand-four-hundred. That's the number of seconds you're given each day. No more. No less. Time is truly your most precious and finite commodity. You can't expand that account. You can't borrow some from yesterday or tomorrow. You can't save some for a day when you really need more. It just doesn't work that way.

There is no way to know how many days, and therefore how many of these seconds, you will be given in your lifetime. It's impossible to predict. So you must be awake each day with the knowledge that the seconds are limited. Accept that you will never get this day back, it can never be re-lived (*Groundhog Day* with Bill Murray shows otherwise, but I hate to break it to you, that movie is not based on a true story). You also can't guard those seconds. Trying to hold onto them doesn't stop time from flowing.

So what must you do? Be cognizant of the passing of time. Don't let the minutes flutter by without attempting to enrich the day for yourself and for others.

If you simply take the time to realize that you will never get your seconds back, you would probably not waste so many. I'm not saying you need to be working gung-ho all the time, but realize your time on this Earth is not infinite. Accept that time is always moving forward, and you can make each tick of the clock more deeply meaningful and more substantial if you want to. When you acknowledge that you are not immortal, and in fact keep your mortality in mind, you can take in the beauty around you more fully. You can do more with the seconds you are given. Even if some of those seconds are spent watching *SpongeBob*, at least acknowledge you won't be in that very spot at that exact time in space ever again. And when you look at it that way, even that annoying sponge can be seen as beautiful.

The flip side (there is ALWAYS a flip side) is that you can't try to squeeze as much as possible into the seconds either. "Enriching" doesn't always equate to "doing more." In the book, *Tools of Titans* by, Tim Ferris, he sums up a ton of interviews he did with some of the most influential, inspiring and successful people on the planet. The book is broken down into three categories: Wealth, Health and Wisdom (though they all intermingle). It's great because each section contains bite-sized chapters. He takes some of the best gems from each interview and puts them on paper. Easy to read, gets the mojo going, and tons of information is right at your fingertips. It only takes a few minutes to read each chapter, but each section definitely makes those minutes more impactful. The flip side (again, there is always a flip side) is I found myself getting overwhelmed by all the amazing things I can try, do, read, and watch to improve my own time on this Earth. There is a plethora of information and activities and knowledge that I can apply, and I found myself thinking "should" rather than "can" as far as the implementation goes. It can be daunting. I only have _____ many seconds left in my life, how can I do all of these things?! I found myself wanting to read, experience, and learn them all by next Wednesday at 5:45 p.m., so that I could tell my family about it over dinner. That is not using the time I have on this planet to the fullest.

You can slow the feeling of time by enriching your seconds. Do one thing right now that will improve your life for however many seconds you have left. Also realize that you don't need to try to uni-cycle, juggle, flambé, meditate, orate, and brush your teeth all at the same time. That would actually get quite messy.

Know that you have a limited span in life, and own that fact. Work to make each second count (for the sake of that second), and don't try to fill the seconds up with as many things as you possibly can.

I'm sure you've heard of the stones in a jar exercise. But even so, here it is again, in a nutshell: Say you have a glass, and beside it you have some larger stones, some pebbles, and some sand. If you wanted "to get as much in as possible" you could start with the sand and fill it up, then move to the pebbles, and then the rocks. Except, there wouldn't be much room for the rocks. If you start with the rocks, and then the pebbles and then sand, the sand can fill in the cracks. The point being, start with the big things first. What can you do with your seconds today that will make your day, week, month, life that much better in the future? Are your rocks spending more time with your family? Working on your health? Practicing your guitar riffs so that you may rock the stage at Red Rocks one day? Getting better at baking your soon-to-be patent-ed Almond Butter Cupcakes that will surely land you a spot on the Home Baking Network? Whatever the big things in your day (meaning, the big things you strive for in life) are, focus on those things first. Fill your time with the most impactful things, not the idle things that keep you from moving toward your goals. You can always add in the small grains of sand later. Define your rocks, fo-cus on those today (and every day) and your seconds will add up to a much more meaningful existence.

The same goes for working on your inner demons- the things holding you back from transformation. You need to eliminate some of the largest distractions and unnecessary time consumers in your life. Contrary to popular opinion, the biggest rocks you can eliminate are in the here and now. I don't think you need to necessarily start with your past. There is no need to start with figuring out or naming the thorns that are poking your flesh. I think one of the best ways to start this journey of elimination is to work on being happy in the present. Start with things that get you going, today. You will most certainly need to address your past at some point, to gleam some reasoning of why you are the way you are. But starting with who you are now is so much more impactful than going back to who you were before as a starting point. When you can gain inspiration in your current life, you can then begin to work on the negative stones holding you back. In life, what matters most is your reactions and your activities in the present, not in the past. So let's get back to THIS moment.

Undoubtedly, you have had the experience of being so deeply immersed in a task/thought/activity that time just seems to disappear. What about the feeling of being so disconnected from said activity that the hands on the clock seem to be stuck, like the clock isn't ticking at all? The first example is what psychologists call being in "flow." It's being completely absorbed in what you're doing, so much so that you lose sense of space and time. Pretty cool, huh? When you're in a state of flow, you know that you will complete your task, and you're having a great time doing it. Time becomes irrelevant. When you're in flow, your goals will be achieved, challenges will be overcome, and satisfaction will be attained. Getting into the flow state both extends time (because you can do whatever the task may be in the time allotted) and simultaneously shortens time (because it just seems to fly by). You don't need to be working on some life-altering amazing project in order to experience flow, either. Think about when you spend time with your best friend, just sit on the porch with your spouse, or whatever it is you're into (some things you can keep to yourself). When you're with them, time flies, you're in flow. The great news is, you have the capacity to get into flow whenever you want. When you combine your passion with whatever you are doing at this instant, you will find yourself in flow.

Another note about time: you are probably going to live longer than you ever thought you would. The fastest growing age demographic is the segment of those 65 years and older. People are living much longer than they did in previous generations. Which is great, unless you weren't planning on living that long. Your grandparents (your reference material for "old age"), very likely passed away at a younger age than you will. This is not an excuse handed to you on a golden pillow, or on a golden pond for that matter.

My intention here is not to fuel the "Well, then, I have plenty of time to get to following my purpose and living an inspiring life" argument. I doubt you need any help in that arena anyway, you are probably plenty good at procrastinating already. The goal is for you to realize that you need to get busy living the life that you were born to live NOW, so that you can fully appreciate all the time you have, and the world can bask in the light you provide during that time. You need to get immersed in your life so you can flow through it.

You also need to get to work on taking care of yourself physically, emotionally, and spiritually, or you will have a lot more time wallowing and feeling less than ideal in those categories. The world is rife with people who are battling pain, illness, and just plain suffering in their 70s, simply due to the fact that they didn't take care of themselves decades before. Read. Write. Learn. Exercise. Get adjusted (shameless Chiropractic plug). Sing. Dance. Smile. Improve your health NOW, so the future will be all the more exciting.

The fact is, you may live longer than you thought, but it's up to you to ensure that those "extra" years are filled with inspiration, health, positivity, and joy, because I can assure you, if you don't put in the work to create those years, you may find that extra time is full of emotional and physical aches and pains.

Get to work on your life. Realize the sooner you head out on this journey, the more "golden" those years will be!

Get your passion to work for you, create and then go with the "flow." Get to work removing the big stones that hold you down, and replace them with the gems that will propel you into being who you're meant to be for the rest of your life. Use the seconds you have each day to expand your love, your creativity, your life, and realize that time is definitely on your side.

PURPOSELY POSITIVE EXERCISE: THE TEST OF TIME

Do the following:

- Grab a friend—

- Or just stand in front of the mirror.

- Look at each other—or the handsome devil in the aforementioned mirror.

- Start a timer for ten minutes—cell phone timer, stopwatch, egg timer, whatever floats your fancy.

- Say nothing. Don't try to make each other (or yourself) laugh.

- Just stand there staring.

- Feel the agony.

- You're not allowed to fall asleep.

- You can't sit down. You just need to stand there (if you have a bad back or knees, or ankles, etc., then, yes, you can sit down and stare, but you need to do that the whole time).

- Notice how INCREDIBLY long ten minutes is.

- Think of all the things your mind was telling you to do instead—what could have you accomplished in that time?

- What IMPORTANT task(s) could you have completed?

- What could you have thoroughly enjoyed in those ten minutes?

- Now realize that segment of time was only ten minutes in a day where you get 1,440 minutes—there's plenty of time for everything you want to do and accomplish, but you must use your time wisely.

PRESSURE-COOKED?

"No beating yourself up over small bumps in the road. Learn to enjoy and appreciate the process. This is especially important because you are going to spend far more time on the actual journey than with those all too brief moments of triumph at the end."

—*Coach Sommer*
(*printed in Tools of Titans, by, Tim Ferris*)

"One way to get high blood pressure is to go mountain climbing over molehills."

—Earl Wilson

Desire. Drive. Motivation. Inspiration. These are all 100% necessary in order to reach your goals, follow your purpose and to allow your passion to flourish. Sometimes, these things bring a friend along for the ride: pressure. Pressure can be a good thing (I'm pretty sure the women of the world would much rather have a diamond engagement ring than one made of coal), but in excess it can be an enormous anchor.

In your attempts to improve your life-to follow your dreams (or to create them as you go along) you can, and undoubtedly will, experience enormous pressure. Pressure from outside sources either saying what you're doing is a waste of time, or saying it's imperative so do it, but by this Friday at noon. You will have pressures from current jobs, your family, your coaching duties, your friends, your enemies, and all those in-between. Pressure is everywhere. However, the largest source of pressure comes from within your very own self.

If you Google (or Bing, or Yahoo, or whatever search engine you use, I don't play favorites) "Pressure Quotes," you will get a ton of results. Line after line of how athletes rise above the pressure, how pressure forged their career through the pressure, etc. It's truly admirable to look into these histories. The problem manifests when you put enormous pressure on yourself to succeed in whatever you're doing, and to succeed RIGHT NOW. You are sabotaging your progress when you demand immediate results.

The true success stories are people who realize there is always pressure externally, but their motivation to do what it takes to achieve the victory was internal.

For example, we look at the pressure of winning the Super Bowl and wonder how these superstar athletes handle it, but we forget the motivation they had as high schoolers to hit the weights, to train, to practice, and to prepare. We discuss the pressure of the final floor routine in the Olympics but neglect to remember the motivation the gymnast had to increase flexibility on a daily basis, to eat right, to exercise. It's easy to forget the inspiration they had to continue to improve. The pressure isn't in the finish line that is a culmination. True pressure is in the preparation.

In fact, sports psychologists have been studying the pressure to succeed for decades. Even more so, a large focus has been placed on the dreaded "choke." In the AFC Championship, January 2012, The Baltimore Ravens trailed the New England Patriots 23 to 20. Billy Cundiff, the Ravens' kicker, was sent onto the field to kick a makable thirty-two-yard field goal to send the game into overtime. He made numerous kicks from that distance before. This time was just a bit different.

Most kickers, and he was no exception, have a routine they go through to get prepared for a big kick. They do certain things on first, second and third down to prepare for their moment. In this game, the scoreboard showed third-down when it was really the fourth-down, so Cundiff was off on his preparation. They rushed him onto the field to score the potential game-tying three points. The pressure placed on him was great, due to the situation, and add into that the sudden change, and elimination of certain aspects of his preparation, and Cundiff was definitely "off." The pressure was a bit too much, and he sailed the kick wide left. The Ravens lost the game and were knocked out of the playoffs.

Another infamous example occurred on April 14, 1996. Golfer, Greg Norman, held a six-shot lead over Nick Faldo going into the final round of the Masters Tournament. The night prior to the final round, Norman was so wound up, he admitted (years later) that he "didn't sleep a wink." The next day, he performed so badly he conceded eleven strokes and lost to Nick Faldo by five.

There is such pressure on 'achieving' that we may lose track of what it takes to just be in the right place for the finish line to appear. The weight of ultimate victory has incapacitated an innumerable amount of people along the way. Billy Cundiff and Greg Norman were both excellent in their fields. They both had successfully completed what they were hoping to complete thousands of times in the past. It wasn't that they hadn't kicked a 32-yard field goal or played a single round of golf before. It was the pressure to succeed in that moment, to come through with a large success/hurdle, which caused them to choke. The pressure of success in those instances outweighed all the time and effort they put into getting there in the first place.

What if you look at it differently? What if you decided the JOURNEY was really the pinnacle of what you're doing. Your "why" cannot be tied to the gold medal or the best snickerdoodle ever (it can be veiled as such, certainly). If you look at those as your ultimate results, realize your TRUE goal is in becoming worthy of attaining these things, and the only way you can do so is by accepting the pressure, by allowing it to help mold and not destroy. The pressure is in the preparation, in working toward an ultimate goal.

The pressure is there, no matter what. However, the gnawing of motivation, the impulse of inspiration is almost always more formidable. Look pressure in the face and combat it with your "why."

The compulsion to succeed is not placed on the victory, it's in the development.

Accept, and therefore, climb over the pressure, and suddenly, rather than holding you back, that same pressure propels you forward. Geysers, rockets and volcanoes are propelled by virtue of the pressure behind them. The weight will always have a place, but it's up to you whether you let it hold you down, or change your view and allow its purpose to spur you onward.

Take some time to look at the loads stacked up "against you." Instead, realize those stresses are there to aid you in your journey. When you can look at the challenges in this regard, you will embrace them with gratitude and understand that, without these pressures, you wouldn't have the fuel to achieve your highest calling.

PURPOSELY POSITIVE EXERCISE: PRESSURE SAVER

Do the following:

- Take a glass out of your cupboard.

- Grab a paper towel or napkin. Write a huge goal of yours on it and then crumple it up.

- Shove that paper towel/napkin into the bottom of the glass

- Make sure you pack it tight enough so that it won't fall out when you turn the glass upside down.

- Now fill a sink or a bucket with water.

- The depth of the water should be at least as deep as your chosen glass.

- Place the glass upside down (straight down) into the water.

- Take the glass out of the water, remove the paper towel/napkin and notice how it's still dry.

- The air pressure in the glass pushed the towel up, and kept it away from the water.

- Realize that pressures in life can help you and they can keep you out of harm's way.

COMPARISON CORRUPTS

"Comparison is an act of violence against the self."

—IYANLA VANZANT

"Comparison is the thief of joy."

—THEODORE ROOSEVELT

How many times do you find yourself looking at someone else's life, job, family, house, car, clothes, sandwiches (maybe not sandwiches as much, but I'm sure it happens), and think, "I wish I had that?" You can sit and look out into the world and compare/contrast with anything and everything you see. Almost all the time you will choose something or someone you PERCEIVE is "better" or "more successful" or a house/car/thing that has a price tag higher than the "thing" you are comparing it to. That may be human nature, especially in a capitalistic society where those dang Joneses make keeping up an eternal battle. However, when you compare, you only push yourself lower. It's like you're grading yourself on some imaginary scale, and you almost always place yourself lower on the curve than the thing/person you're comparing to.

When you judge yourself against the vastness of the human race, there will always be someone or something that is *"better"* than you are. Those people, in turn, will find the exact same conundrum if/when they play the comparison game. There will always be flaws to point out when you look through your lenses at others. At best, that vision is blurry and often distorted. You see what you **perceive** to be true. You get a snapshot in time, but you don't see the entire picture. That fact alone makes the comparison unfair (to you and to them).

There was an experiment of sorts rampaging through social media a while back. An image of a dress was posted and you had to discern if it was black and white or blue and gold. People went crazy over it. Many people swore it was black and white, many swore blue and gold. Your perception of the color drove your "reality" of it. The truth is: your perception is unique to you.

Imagine you see a beautiful family of four in the airport. They're laughing, smiling, excited for their upcoming trip to Fiji (probably their fourteenth time there or something). The entire family is well-dressed, the children are making adoring comments to each other and to their parents. Their luggage is impeccable, and definitely costs more than what you're hauling around. In the background, your children's voices break through, *"Dad, Joey is being a butthead!" "No I'm not! Sally kicked me in the leg with her suitcase and she's a fart-knocker!" "Well that's only because Joey's slow and he's blocking up traffic."* Your wife chimes in, *"This is all because you're a horrible, horrible person, husband, and father..."* O.K. that is taking it a bit far (and that kind of voice actually, more often than not, comes from inside your own mind), but can you picture this situation? You could very easily make the snap decision that the other family has definitely has "got their stuff" together more than you do. They are a happier family. They are just better people. I'm pretty sure that, since you're old enough to read, you have by now realized that snap decisions are rarely the best way to determine a path. When you compare your life to the twenty-second (or twenty-minute or twenty-hour or even twenty-year) interval of another human being, you are exponentially comparing apples to orangutans.

When you compare yourself to others, you are negating who you truly are. You're not and can never be anyone but yourself. If you're experiencing internal struggle, and you think (for the moment) that you're not worth much, and that person over there is the "gold standard," how in the world does that HELP you? Can you magically bump up against them and by osmosis take in everything they are? Can you breathe in their exhalations and fill the holes you've created within? Can you replicate their lives 100% by following them through the airport, sitting in their car, replicating their walk? (The answer is a definite NO, and in actuality, doing those things are most likely a one-way trip to creepy-town and/or incarceration, which would be counterproductive). You cannot become anyone else except you, even if you breathe in the contents of a magical famous-people breath receptacle (a guy sold canisters of breath from actors at the Oscars for a lot of money on eBay—no joke). But you can continually adapt who you are. You can improve, you can stay the same, or you can devolve.

I think it is so important to learn from others. I read a plethora of book, listen to podcasts from people I admire, watch inspirational videos, and am continually on the look-out for learning opportunities. I have also made many mistakes in thinking, "I want to be just like _____." The reason for those desires have been steeped in comparison. I have found it is tremendously beneficial to learn from others, but also tremendously detrimental to think I need to *become* them. For a large portion of my life—even though I now practice gratitude daily—I was still looking at what others had, who (I thought) they were, their successes, their accolades, their family, their (fill-in-the-blank, and comparing all of these (fill-in-the-blanks) to my life, to who I was, to what I had, and so on and so on. As a child, I laughed at the "keeping up with the Jones" mantra. Once I realized the meaning of the phrase, I still thought it was pretty idiotic. *"How could I compare to another family? I don't really know them at all."* Somewhere through time, I lost that feeling. I started stacking myself up against others. You would think this mental measuring up would be in order to hold myself higher. One would think it would be to prove to myself that I was in fact "doing great." The sad thing is, the exact opposite was my truth. I was comparing myself to others in order to prove that I have "a long way to go." I was stacking myself up, just so I could see that I was nowhere near where I "needed" to be. I was, essentially, a toddler. I was stacking up a column of wood blocks just so I could knock them down.

You live in an age where learning is, quite literally, at your fingertips. You can Google any number of gurus: successful people, authors, musicians, and can read their story. You can scroll through accolades of anyone you wish. There is an infinite number of columns you can compare your stack of blocks to. This is not a bad thing. The problem isn't the internet, or the plethora of information that you have access to. Because, you don't even need tablets, phones or computers to feed the comparison monster. You can simply glance across the street at your neighbor's new car, or their lawn, or the ropes course they built in the backyard for their children.

The problem is when you start comparing your *existence* to theirs. There is a phrase, and I can't remember who coined it, (maybe Tupac) but it goes something like this: "They hate us 'cause they ain't us." I think we could easily move some words around to something like, "you dislike yourself because you ain't them" (I know it definitely doesn't have the same flow or cadence). You impose restrictions upon yourself, and these restrictions have a strong foundation in how you "measure up" to others.

Additionally, comparison with others isn't very fair to them. You're looking at them through rose-colored glasses. Chances are, the person you see isn't the *real* them anyway. They most likely, wouldn't be able to live up to your perception of them, either.

By all means, learn from others. Admire people who've done what you want to do. Be proud of your neighbor's accolades and their successes (and their ropes courses). There is nothing wrong with noticing how amazing the people you share your time with on this planet truly are. Be aware of all the awesomeness that the human race has and will accomplish.

I'm merely proposing you take a step back and try not to immediately get out your measuring stick to see where you stack up against them. Learn, but also realize that their path is different than yours. Don't try to "win" against them. That's like trying to beat a bowler while you're playing checkers; they are completely different games.

The only person you should truly compare yourself to is the person you see in the mirror (when no one else is in the room). If you work on improving yourself for the sake of improvement only (not to gain in an imaginary race against the world), I can promise you life will be exorbitantly more satisfying, and you will look back at that competition and know you made an impact on your family, friends, community, and the world.

PURPOSELY POSITIVE EXERCISE: CHARACTER COMPARISON

Grab your notebook and do the following:

1. Call to mind your favorite sitcom—*Friends*? *Cheers*? *Roseanne*? *The Big Bang Theory*? The Good Place? It doesn't matter.

2. Pick two of the main characters in the show and write a list comparing and contrasting them—their height, their hair color and length, their weight, their laughter, their jobs, their mannerisms, etc.

3. Make the lists long and in depth.

4. Now realize what a huge waste of time this activity was–as the companions have done nothing for you.

5. Then try this activity instead—write a list of all the ways you're different (for the better) than you were in Middle School or High School.

6. Take time to think about how much a different, upgraded person you are now.

7. Make sure you think about the un-measurables, such as love, passion, purpose, integrity, friendship.

8. If you think about it, to truly compare something you need to be able to quantify it.

9. In life, some of the very best things are not "measurable," which means these things cannot be quantified with numbers.

10. I'm sure you can easily see the growth you've achieved in your life compared to who you were when you were younger. Comparison only matters if you're comparing yourself to...yourself.

BEST-SELFIE

"Never stop doing your best just because someone doesn't give you credit."

—Zack Lee

"When you look in the mirror what do you see in yourself? You should see survival, greatness, passion, hunger and faith. You are a conqueror, so put on your best look and be great."

—Alton Gatling Jr.

A pparently, "selfies" are all the rage. People love taking pictures of themselves, or with their friends, through the tiny camera on the front of their smartphones. I've even offered to take the picture for the happy couple in front of the backdrop of the Rocky Mountains, and more often than not, they kindly decline and want to shoot the pic themselves. That may just be due to lack of faith in my photographical ability, but still... Have you ever given thought to what your best self would look like?

If you could take a selfie of your best self, and then had the ability to look at that image, and dissect it for all it's worth, what would that person look/feel/think/act like? It's actually a wonderful exercise.

Take some time today to sit in peace and picture the very best version of yourself. It may be easier to do so by imagining yourself twenty years in the future. Go deep with this exercise. What do you look like? Where do you live? How is your home decorated? What's your demeanor? How're you dressed? What do you offer yourself as a beverage for the conversation you're about to have?

When you make an effort to visualize the best you have to offer, you will know what you're working toward. You can ask your ideal self for advice or for the knowledge needed to bridge the gap between who you are now and who your best self is. What do you need to do/think less of, and what do you need to incorporate more of into your life now?

The distance between the present you and the ideal you may be large, or it may seem incredibly small, but by taking time to sit with your ideal self, you can see the journey as surmountable.

"A journey of a thousand miles begins with a single step."

—Laozi (Chinese Philosopher Circa 531).

In order to become who you truly want to become, you need to see who that is, and then take the first step toward meeting him/her (every day). It's also beneficial to touch base with your best self when you feel stuck, low, or need advice. I'm not suggesting you walk around the light-rail station mumbling to your best self in an interview scenario. I think it would be best served to do so in the comfort of your own home, but in all honesty, whatever you need to do to keep the vision strong–go for it! Who cares what the other passengers on the train think anyway?

I have done this exercise numerous times (I first discovered it from a mediation application called Insight Timer), and it has been extremely beneficial. When you do this exercise, it's completely acceptable to visualize all the "things" your best self has (nice home, amazing vehicle, etc.) but it is even more important to notice their personality, their traits, their demeanor, their presence. Those last the longest and make the biggest impact on the world.

The key is to know who you can become, not only the stuff you can accumulate.

Your day will be filled with an unfathomable amount of decisions. You decide what you're going to wear, what you're going to eat for breakfast, if you want to wash your hair or not, how you're going to make your bed, maybe even whether you'll get out of bed at all, or make a huge plate of nachos, bring them back to bed and fall asleep in the sour cream.

And all of those decisions take place within the first hour or so of your day. Think about how many other decisions you make daily. Some are small, some have a much larger impact on your day/week/month/life.

We had a meeting in December of 2017 with some amazing Chiropractors and Chiropractic Assistants. The purpose of these meetings was to learn, to connect and to improve how we serve our patients. A friend of mine (and great Chiropractor, Dave Orlando, D.C.) stated something along the lines of, "*We have a battle every day. The battle is between who we were that got us to where we are right now, and who we want to be who will take us where we want to go. It's about deciding which person we want to fight alongside with.*" I loved this. The fact is, you truly are a conglomerate of your previous selves. You are what you habitually do, think and act. You are the result of all of those decisions you've made up until today. So who you will be twenty years from now will be the result of the next twenty years of decisions, plus who you are right now. That same night after the aforementioned meeting, I received this email (from a service called *Notes From The Universe*) "*Everyone, Joel, lives the life of their choosing. Not just what they chose, but what they are choosing.*" And then before bed, I read this in the book, *The Miracle* Morning, "*...all that matters is that you and I are committed to leaving the past in the past and making our lives exactly the way we want them to be, starting today.*"

Sensing a theme here? I took that as a "nudge" (discussed previously in this book) that I really need to delve into my daily decisions. I needed to make more of a conscious effort to notice all the decisions I make, and look at them through the lens of my best self.

How would he choose? Which road would he take? Which snack would he eat? Which book would he read next? Would he just lay in bed today?

Implement this into your week. Get to know your best self. Realize that your best self is you, just further along in the journey. Work on getting a clear "selfie" of that person. When you know who you were born to be (or at least when you take steps to try to understand that person), then you have a path to travel toward. Start taking that first step every day in becoming who you you were born to be, who the world needs you to be. Because you aren't supposed to become your ideal self just for your own sake. Doing so will improve your own life tremendously, but even more so, becoming who you were meant to be will improve the entire world.

PURPOSELY POSITIVE EXERCISE: PICTURE PAGE

Do the following:

- Get out your colored pencils, stencils, 10,000-color Crayon box, whatever your art weapon of choice is.

- Draw, in great detail, your future awesome you, including:

  ○ Where you live.

  ○ Your job.

  ○ Your spouse.

  ○ Your car.

  ○ Your friends.

- If you can't draw some of the things, just make fancy words or write out what your ideal life includes.

- Picture your life as beautiful (it is).

A VIBRANT PEACE?

"The greatest self is a peaceful smile, that always sees the world smiling back."

—Bryant H McGill

"If we are peaceful, if we are happy, we can smile, and everyone in our family, our entire society, will benefit from our peace."

—Thich That Hanh

Vibrant and peaceful. At first glance, these two words can almost seem like opposites. However, they definitely aren't. In fact, I believe you need to bring both words to the forefront to work in harmony, in order to live a fulfilled life. Let's examine these words in a bit more detail, shall we? (Not really fair to ask you, because that's exactly what we're going to do in the next few paragraphs, so if your answer is "No," then I advise you to skip ahead a bit).

According to *dictionary.com*, there are a quite a few definitions of the word vibrant, many having to do with music and vibrations. There are two, however that I would like to focus on: "pulsating with vigor and energy," and "vigorous; energetic; vital."

When you are truly alive, living your purpose, living with inspiration, you are pulsating with energy and vigor. You are energetic and vital. I bet when you think of the word "vital" it sparks a warm feeling inside, and possibly a yearning to be a bit more of that word. People are naturally attracted to vibrant individuals. They exude positivity. They demonstrate confidence. They're naturally "likable." When you are vibrant, things are definitely on the "up and up." Sounds like a pretty good word to emulate, right?

How about peaceful? Again, *dictionary.com* defines peaceful as: peaceable; not argumentative, quarrelsome, or hostile.

Seems like a pretty good definition, but I think we can delve a bit deeper (yes, in this instance I'm saying I may know more than *dictionary.com*, you can't trust everything on the internet anyway, right?). When I think of peace, I think of comfort, calm, tranquility, harmony, amicable, etc. When you think of peace, what do you picture?

I think you can agree that "peace" is a positive word. Peaceful is a positive, desirous state of being. People who are at peace are not easily shaken. They are solid, they exude a comfort to those around them and to their surroundings. When you're following your purpose, when you're truly inspired, you're at ease and living peacefully.

Let's combine these two: vibrant peace (or maybe peaceful vibrancy). Picture living with purpose, striving toward improvement but with a sense of calm and comfort about the journey. You are pulled (more than pushed) toward pursuing your best self because it feels so good to do so. You feel compelled to live with enthusiasm, and drive through a smooth, steady path. (That is not to say there won't be bumps, or hurdles, or walls. It's just that you're at peace with the knowledge they will be there, but your vibrancy trumps your obstacles).

Live to improve. Follow your heart strings. Allow your soul to tug you toward living a more impactful life, most definitely. However, do so with peace in mind, knowing that following your inspiration is the highest level of your life. You are destined to do so. The drive should also produce some solace if you're truly allowing inspiration to drive.

Go forth. Be vibrant. Be at peace.

PURPOSELY POSITIVE EXERCISE: PEACEFUL PORTIONS*

Consider the following:

- When do you feel most at peace during your day?
  - Waking up?
  - Sitting with your coffee?
  - Just before bed?
  - While you're asleep?
- Notice how your most peaceful times actually help build up a reservoir of energy—be mindful of these times and think about how you can incorporate some peace into your day every day in order to revitalize!

DARE TO
BE GREAT—DARE TO
BE YOU

"Success isn't a result of spontaneous combustion. You must set yourself on fire."

—Arnold H Glasow

"God gives us dreams a size too big so that we can grow into them."

—Unknown

Lloyd Dobler sits uncomfortably in his shirt and tie, discussing his possible future with the High School Guidance Counselor. When asked what he wants to do with his future, he responds with a long-winded statement that he doesn't want anything to do with sales, buying or processing, but then he says, "I'm looking for a dare-to-be-great situation."[1] What an amazing statement. I think we are all looking for the same. I, like many of the world's population, love reading/watching/listening to inspirational stories about people overcoming tragedy, misfortune, illness, death, etc. I get fired up hearing about people who pick themselves up from the

---

1. Say Anything the movie, Cameron Crowe

depths to keep moving forward, accomplishing great tasks and changing the world. The trouble is, I think many of us are waiting for that dare-to-be-great situation, and not working on just being great.

Everyone in the world will go through struggles, but not everyone (thankfully) will go through horrendous tragedy. You probably won't be stuck, pinned between rocks on a hiking trip and have to decide to cut your own arm off for survival (The Aaron Ralston story). You probably won't have a life-threatening injury just before getting drafted into the NFL, lose the function of an arm, and have to change your life forever (Inky Johnson). I'd wager you won't find yourself on a plane hijacked by terrorists with deadly intent, and have to decide to muster up the courage to tell others, "Let's roll," and sacrifice yourself for the sake of a nation (*The Story of Flight 93*). Odds are you will not find yourself in these types of situations.

That doesn't mean you get to wade through life until a situation such as this comes up and challenges you. Forge your character. You don't need a cataclysmic defining moment in order to be great. Be great now.

I know that in my life, I may not be fighting enemies, or warding off evil spirits that threaten to invade my home. But I do know that every single day I have a wife and two children who depend on me. I know that I will affect the lives of more than one-hundred people a day. I know that there are people who look up to me. I know there are people I need to learn from. I know that if I sit around half-invested in my life as it is now, hoping for a situation that pulls out the very best in me, one that is worthy of amazing stories, one that is forever encapsulated in the annals of history as an true pinnacle of courage and inspiration... I may just sit in my recliner and wait around forever.

My (and your) dare-to-be-great situation is EVERY situation. Character isn't only forged in the situations that test us. Character is *brought out* fully in them, but not created. Your character is created in how you live your life in every moment. Your courage is *tested* in tough times, but it's learned and generated in how you live your life each and every day.

The true challenge is to show up as the best version of you (or at least the best version of who you can be that day) every day. Recognize the impact you have on your family, friends, strangers, the entire world, and own that impact and its sanctity. True greatness is created from the moment you get up and brush your teeth until the moment you go to bed. Live today as your best self. Dare to be great!

> *"You beat cancer by how you live, why you live and the manner in which you live."*
>
> —STUART SCOTT

If you haven't had the opportunity to do so, please do yourself a favor and watch Stuart Scott's acceptance speech of the Jimmy V. Award on ESPN.[2] If you have seen it, still, go there and watch it now. It's only about eight-minutes-long, but it's profound in message about living life, fighting for life, and the reasons to do so.

You may not be fighting cancer right now. You are probably fighting any other type of terminal illness. You are not constantly pushing and clawing to close death's door. You may not be wrestling yourself from the jaws of an alligator for survival, but I can say with absolute conviction that you (along with everyone else on this planet) are fighting your inner demons.

You're trying to improve, to make an impact, to do the best you can with what you have, to thrive. At the end of life, the stories recorded (written, verbal, or in the form of memories) will be based upon how you lived, why you lived, and the manner in which you lived.

Your "accomplishments" will be footnotes. Dates, times and places will be recorded for posterity, but your character will design the narrative. Who you are will determine so much more than

---

2. *http://www.nydailynews.com/sports/video-espn-stuart-scott-delivers-emtional-espys-speech-article-1.1870323*

what you do. The way you go about life, how you influence others, the quality of the connections you make, those will determine your legacy.

You may not have direct control over the obstacles you will face, but you do have within your grasp the ability to respond to whatever is placed in front of you. You have the power to forge your days, to determine what will propel you forward, to seek out the "whys" in life. You are blessed with the gift of conscious thought and the ability to construct and reconstruct who you are at any given time.

So choose to look at life differently. Change your perspective in order to determine who you want to become, and live in a manner consistent with that vision. You get to decide. It's ALWAYS up to you to create a life of importance and to impact others in a profoundly positive way.

You get to love. You get to care. Every day you can work on forging your masterpiece for the good of all those who witness it. Whether you admit it or not, you matter to so many people in this beautiful world, and you get to do your part to leave it a bit more breathtaking with each breath you are blessed to have upon it.

So as Stuart Scott said, *"Our life's journey is about the people who touch us."* That works both ways. You will touch a lot of people while living. It's up to you who you will be in all of those instances. You can either wake up each day, accept mediocrity and merely drift. Or you can truly live. You can accept the responsibility to impact the world and to bring forth the light. You get to make that choice, every day.

I sincerely hope that in reading this book, you have caught the notion that you can look at life differently. Where you are in life right now is a summation of all the thoughts, attitudes, and experiences you've had up until this moment. You can improve your future by changing your perspective, making different decisions, and realizing that only you can author your legacy. Additionally, I hope that through the PPEs, you're able to get in touch with your spirit, begin to feel that ache, that urging to improve, and you get busy becoming who you're meant to be.

Part of that desire is selfish. I know the world can only be truly amazing if all the truly amazing people in it get in touch with their truly amazing selves and start sharing that with the world. You see, I KNOW that you're one-of-a-kind. No one in this entire universe can do you like you can. You're worth it. You're supposed to live an inspired life, and quite frankly, the rest of us deserve to see how amazing you really are.

"When a man, for whatever reason, has the opportunity to lead an extraordinary life, he has no right to keep it to himself."—**Jacques Yves Coustou**

You have the opportunity to lead an extraordinary life. This doesn't necessarily mean you will find cures for cancer, win Nobel Prizes, eliminate hunger, pitch in multiple World Series games, or create the best BBQ recipe ever made. But that also doesn't let you off the hook.

You can and should live a life that is truly extraordinary. You can catapult mediocrity. You can live intentionally to inspire, achieve, love deeply, and embolden others. You can provide hope and compassion. You can allow your soul to grow luminescent for the world to see, and gain comfort from its glow. You can be the very best version of you and shine as bright as possible. And when you do, I guarantee, the world will be in awe of your brilliance.

Shakespeare once wrote: "All the world's a stage, and all the men and women merely players." (*As You Like It, Act I Scene VII*) This may be true, but players we are still. Complacency breeds negativity. Status quo stifles inspiration. In order to paint our lives with vibrant hope and positivity, we must participate in it fully. Our lives will not improve if we are idle. The anchors, the weights in our souls will not lighten their load through inaction. We only remove those shackles through conscious, directed effort. We must strive to color our lives with positivity, passion and purpose. Become who you want to be. Create the life you deserve.

Craft your legacy. You are its master sculptor and we all anxiously await your masterpiece.

PURPOSELY POSITIVE EXERCISE: DOUBLE-DOG-DARE YOU!

Congratulations! You have finished this book. Now I have a challenge for you:

- Go back through and revisit PPEs in this book for the next few weeks, before you move on to another book—take time to redo these exercises again, because the answers, pictures, processes will change as you do.

- Work on your mind.

- Nurture your soul.

- Bring your best self to the world—we will ALL be grateful!

INDEX OF INSPIRATION

Need some nudging along your path to your positively inspiring life? Is assistance needed to help flip the switch from the natural state of negativity to being purposefully positive? Simply need some gas in your inspiration engine? Here is a list (not all-inclusive, this is not Cancun) of resources that have helped me along my path (in no particular hierarchical order). Feel free to message me at *AuthorJoelLindeman@gmail.com with more suggestions as well!*

BOOKS

Tools of Titans —Tim Ferris

The Energy Bus —Jon Gordon

The Carpenter —Jon Gordon

The Positive Dog —Jon Gordon

The Power of a Positive Team —Jon Gordon

The Motivation Manifesto —Brendon Burchard

High Performance Habits —Brendon Burchard

Life's Golden Ticket: An Inspirational Novel —Brendon Burchard

The Fire Starter Sessions —Danielle LaPorte

The Book of Joy —The Dalai Lama, Desmond Tutu and Douglas Abrams

It's Not About You —Bob Burg

The Go-Giver: A Little Story About a Powerful Business Idea —Bob Burg

The Happiness Advantage —Shawn Achor

You are a Badass: How to Stop Doubting Your Greatness and Start Living an Awesome Life —Jen Sincere

The Prophet —Kahlil Gibran

The Power of Habit: Why We Do What We Do In Life and Business —Chalres Duhigg

The Code of The Extraordinary Mind: 10 Unconventional Laws to Redefine Your Life and Succeed on Your Own Terms —Vishen Lakhiani

Discovering Your Soul Signature: A 33 Day Path to Purpose, Passion and Joy —Penache Desai

Leaders Eat Last —Simon Sinek

Start with Why: How Great Leaders Inspire Everyone to Take Action —Simon Sinek

Think and Grow Rich —Napolean Hill

The 10X Rule: The Only Difference Between Success and Failure —Grant Cardone

Change Your Thoughts-Change Your Life: Living the Wisdom of the Tao —Wayne Dyer

The Power of Intention: Learning to Co-create Your World Your Way —Wayne Dyer

10% Happier: How I Tamed the Voice in My Head, Reduced Stress Without Losing My Edge, and Found Self-Help That Actually Works —Dan Harris

Daring Greatly: How the Courage to Be Vulnerable Transforms the Way We Live, Love, Parent and Lead —Brene Brown

The Alchemist —Paulo Coelho

Breaking the Habit of Being Yourself: How to Lose Your Mind and Create a New One —Joe Dispenza

The Last Lecture —Randy Pausch

The Greatest Salesman in the World —Og Mandino

Man's Search For Meaning —Viktor Frankl

I'll Push You: A Journey of 500 Miles, Two Best Friends, and One Wheelchair —Patrick Gray

The 7 Habits of Highly Effective People —Sean Covey

Good to Great: Why Some Companies Make the Leap—-and Others Don't —Jim Collins

The Five People You Meet In Heaven —Mitch Albom

Tuesdays with Morrie —Mitch Albom

The Richest Man in Babylon —George Samuel Clason

Grit: The Power of Passion and Perseverance —Angela Duckworth

Awaken to Giant Within —Tony Robbins

The Power of Positive Thinking: 10 Traits for Maximum Results —Norman Vicent Peale

Don't Sweat the Small Stuff and It's All Small Stuff: Simple Ways to Keep the Little Things From Taking Over Your Life —Richard Carlson

The Subtle Art of Not Giving a F*ck: A Counterintuitive Approach to Living a Good Life —Mark Manson

Triggers: Creating Behavior That Lasts—Becoming the Person You Want To Be —Marshall Goldsmith

The Book Thief —Markus Zusak

The Art of Racing in the Rain —Garth Stein

For One More Day —Mitch Albom

The Wings of Joy: Finding Your Path to Inner Peace —Sri Chinmoy

The Noticer —Andy Andrews

VIDEOS

https://www.ted.com/talks/shawn_achor_the_happy_secret_to_better_work

https://www.ted.com/talks/brene_brown_on_vulnerability

https://www.ted.com/talks/simon_sinek_how_great_leaders_inspire_action

https://www.ted.com/talks/bj_miller_what_really_matters_at_the_end_of_life

https://www.ted.com/talks/isabel_allende_how_to_live_passionately_no_matter_your_age/transcript

https://www.ted.com/talks/angela_lee_duckworth_grit_the_power_of_passion_and_perseverance

https://www.ted.com/talks/dan_gilbert_asks_why_are_we_happy

https://www.ted.com/talks/norman_lear_an_entertainment_icon_on_living_a_life_of_meaningThe Pursuit of Happyness- 2006

http://www.nydailynews.com/sports/video-espn-stuart-scott-delivers-emtional-espys-speech-article-1.1870323

https://www.youtube.com/watch?v=N6XkvoBhhLI (Vishen Lakhiani on Goal Setting: Redefined)

The Last Lecture by Randy Pausch: *https://www.youtube.com/watch?v=j7zzQpvoYcQ*

Any videos on the site: Soulpancake.com

MOVIES

Invictus Directed by Clint Eastwood, Distributed by Warner Bros Pictures, Dec 11, 2009.

Good Will Hunting Directed by Gus Van Sant, Distributed by Miramax Films, Jan 9, 1998.

Awakenings Directed by Penny Marshall, Distributed by Columbia Pictures, Dec 22, 1990.

Remember the Titans Directed by Boaz Yakin, Distributed by Buena Vista Pictures, Sept 29, 2000.

Life Is Beautiful Directed by Roberto Benigni, Distributed by Miramax Films, Dec 20, 1997.

Million Dollar Baby Directed by Clint Eastwood, Distributed by Warner Bros Pictures, Dec 15, 2004.

Scent of A Woman Directed by Martin Brest, Distributed by Universal Pictures, Dec 23, 1992.

The Blind Side Directed by John Lee Hancock, Distributed by Warner Bros Pictures, Nov 20, 2009.

Rush Directed by Ron Howard, Distributed by Universal Pictures, Sept 27, 2013.

Dead Poets Society Directed by Peter Weir, Distributed by Buena Vista Pictures, June 2, 1989.

My Left Foot Directed by Jim Sheridan, Distributed by Palace Pictures, Feb 24, 1989.

127 Hours Directed by Danny Boyle, Distributed by Fox Searchlight Pictures, Nov 5, 2010.

The Descendants Directed by Aleaxander Payne, Distributed by Fox Searchlight Pictures, Nov 18, 2011.

Chariots of Fire Directed by Hugh Hudson, Distributed by Warner Bros Pictures, March 30, 1981.

The King's Speech Directed by Tom Hooper, Distributed by Momentum Pictures, Sept 6, 2011.

Up Directed by Pete Docter, Distributed by Walt Disney Studios, May 29, 2009.

Boundin' (*Pixar Short*) Directed by Bud Luckey, Distributed by Buena Vista Pictures, Nov 5, 2004 (released with the *The Incredibles*).

Cool Runnings Directed by John Turteltaub, Distributed by Buena Vista Pictures, Oct 1 1993.

Rocky Directed by John G. Avildsen, Distributed by United Artists, Dec 3, 1976.

One Flew Over the Cuckoo's Nest Directed by Milos Forman, Distributed by United Artists, Nov 19, 1975.

Whiplash Directed by Damien Chazelle, Distributed by Sony Pictures Classics, Oct 10, 2014.

Slumdog Millionaire Directed by Danny Boyle, Distributed by Fox Searchlight Pictures, Jan 9 2009.

Escape To Victory Directed by John Huston, Distributed by Paramount Pictures, July 30, 1981.

The Pursuit of Happyness Directed by Gabriele Muccino, Distributed by Columbia Pictures (Sony Pictures releasing), Dec 15, 2006.

The Notebook Directed by Nick Cassavetes, Distributed by New Line Cinema, June 25, 2004.

Reign Over Me Directed by Mike Binder, Distributed by Columbia Pictures, March 23, 2007.

The Greatest Game Ever Played Directed by Bill Paxton, Distributed by Buena Vista Pictures, Sept 30, 2005.

Freedom Writers Directed by Richard LaGravenese, Distributed by Paramount Pictures, Jan 5, 2007.

Miracle Directed by Gavin O' Connor, Distributed by Buena Vista Pictures, Feb 6, 2004.

Lean On Me Directed by John G. Avildsen, Distributed by Warner Bros, Mar 3, 1989.

42 Directed by Brian Helgeland, Distributed by Warner Bros, April 12, 2013.

Big Fish Directed by Tim Burton, Distributed by Columbia Pictures, Dec 10, 2003.

The Green Mile Directed by Frank Darabont, Distributed by Warner Bros, Dec 10, 1999.

Eternal Sunshine of the Spotless Mind Directed by Michel Gondry, Distributed by Focus Features, Mar 19, 2004.

The Way Directed by Emilio Estevez, Distributed by Icon Entertainment International, Oct 7, 2011.

The Help Directed by Tate Taylor, Distributed by Walt Disney Studios, Aug 10, 2011.

The Secret Life of Walter Mitty Directed by Ben Stiller, Distributed by 20th Century Fox Samuel Goldwyn Films, Dec 25, 2013.

Forrest Gump Directed by Robert Zemeckis, Distributed by Paramount Pictures, July 6, 1994.

Braveheart Directed by Mel Gibson, Distributed by Paramount Pictures, May 24, 1995.

It's a Wonderful Life Directed by Frank Capra, Distributed by RKO Radio Pictures, Dec 20, 1946.

Saving Private Ryan Directed by Steven Spielberg, Distributed by Dreamworks Pictures, July 24, 1998.

WEBSITES/SUBSCRIPTIONS

https://training.tonyrobbins.com/the-6-human-needs-why-we-do-what-we-do/

http://www.lifehack.org/articles/work/how-find-meaning-your-job-and-work-happily.html

http://www.oprah.com/spirit/Finding-Meaning-and-Purpose-in-Your-Life

https://www.tonyrobbins.com/mind-meaning: Tony Robbins activity on finding your meaning

https://www.dailyom.com/: Daily Om email service with an article to set the stage for a tremendous day

http://thedragontree.com/: Natural, healthy products and articles/ blogs to boost creativity and inspiration

https://www.tut.com/Inspiration/nftu: Notes from the universe email subscription service

https://oxytocinsite.wordpress.com/: (Daily Inspirational blog with guest contributors)

https://gratitudeforflow.wordpress.com/: (A gratitude blog we use at my office, open to submissions as well)

http://www.coachwooden.com/: Coach John Wooden is one of the most inspirational people ever

www.mindvalley.com: Website with links to meditations, videos and inspirational content

http://www.achievement.org/: brings students visionaries, leaders, and pioneers who have helped shape our world to you

http://www.thesuccessprinciples.com/: Jack Canfield's (author of the Chicken Soup for the Soul series) site *http://storytellersforgood.com/*: Promoting goodness, inspiring greatness

http://soulpancake.com/: Actor Rainn Wilson's site. SoulPancake's mission is to open hearts and minds through smart and hopeful content that uplifts, inspires, and helps us all figure out what it means to be human

https://www.thedolectures.com/: "The idea is a simple one. That the people who do things can inspire the rest of us to go do amazing thigs too."

http://www.daniellelaporte.com/: Author of The Fire Starter Sessions. You can also sign up here for a "daily truth bomb," a service that will send you an inspirational text daily

https://zenhabits.net/: Great daily posts to help motivate and inspire

https://www.happify.com/public/happify-daily/: Website with research, videos, games and more to help boost happiness

SONGS

There are so many amazing songs, so I decided to do something a bit different with this category. Go to Google Play Music and checkout my INSPIRATION playlist (*https://goo.gl/ZT5sAj*). There is a wide variety of musical genres there, but all of these songs help motivate, uplift and inspire. I am hoping that you would like to contribute. I am always on the lookout for more ways to keep my fire going (and to share those ways with others). Feel free to email me at: *AuthorJoelLindeman@gmail.com* with your submissions. I am looking forward to your suggestions!

BALANCING ACT

"I would rather walk with a friend in the dark, than alone in the light."

–Helen Keller

"I have learned that to be with those I like is enough."

—Walt Whitman

There is a fantastic song by the X Ambassadors titled "Unsteady." I loved it the first time I heard it, and all it took was the opening (and often repeated) line: "Hold, hold onto me, because I'm a little unsteady." In reading the words, it actually seems quite pedestrian. But together with the emotion in the song, it tugs at my heart strings. We will all definitely feel unsteady at times, and I am forever grateful for those amazing souls that keep me balanced.

To my wife: You are beauty. You soften the edges of this world, and you illuminate everything you touch. Everyone who has ever met you is a far better person for having done so. Your love is contagious and is exactly what humanity needs. "You are my person, and you are my world!"

To my brother, Tony: You have endured so much in your life, and you always have time for a joke and an uplifting smile to share. You are constantly on the lookout to help others in life, and I am beyond proud to be your brother. Even if you tortured me a bit when we were younger. (We should find time to make up all those one-on-one baseball games I backed out of).

To my sister, Robin: Slightly small in stature but huge in heart. Thank you for your guidance, laughter and friendship. (And for helping me get through my teenage years alive).

To my sister, Karin: We had some rough times when we were younger, but your kindness and logic have helped me in so many ways. I am grateful for our bond. Thank you.

To Payton: Your curiosity for the world and your hunger for knowledge is equalled only by your compassion for others. I cannot wait to see how the world changes for the better due to your impact on it. I am tremendously lucky and overwhelmingly proud to be your father.

To Isaac: Your genuine love for others inspires me every day, and your empathy amazes me. You are a friend to all those who get to know you; your joy is just what the world needs. I am so grateful to be your father and witness your goodness and the light you bring to the world.

To my Mom and Dad: I am so grateful for your love, guidance and support. I know I can be strong-headed at times, yet you have never clipped my wings. You have supported me in all my endeavors and have helped me become the man I am today. I love you both so very much.

To Spike and Mary: Thank you so much for welcoming me into your loving family. The closeness that you and Sheri have is truly wonderful. You have always supported me from the beginning, and I am eternally grateful to be a part of your family.

I have have been incredibly blessed with amazing friends and mentors in my life. I put those two words together (friends and mentors), because in truth they are inseparable. Every single one of you have provided companionship and have helped me grow (and continue to do so) into the person I want to become. There are way too many to mention here, but I hope you know who you are. Much love to every single one of you.

To my editor, Jennifer Blanchard: Thank you for your guidance in piecing together my thoughts into proper flow. Thank you for helping me put commas and spaces and "ies" before "ees." Thank you for helping me create this book. Your assistance has been monumental. Phillip Gessert, my book interior designer, and Ashley Siebels, my book cover designer: Thank you for taking my words and morphing them into art. Lianne Heffelman: I am grateful for your thoughtful feedback and assistance with my early manuscript.

For everyone who has taken the time to read this book. YOU ROCK! The only reason you would have done so is because you have a passion for improving the world. For that, I am profoundly appreciative.